Positive Selfishness

Positive Selfishness

A Practical Guide to Self-Esteem

Frieda Porat, Ph.D.,
with Margery Quackenbush

Celestial Arts
Millbrae, CA

Copyright © 1977 by Freida Porat

Published by CELESTIAL ARTS, 231 Adrian Road, Millbrae,
California 94030

First printing: May, 1977
Manufactured in the United States of America

Library of Congress Cataloging in Publication Data

Porat, Freida, 1925–
    Positive selfishness.

    1. Self-respect.   2. Self-perception.
3. Assertiveness   (Psychology)   I. Quackenbush,
Margery, joint author.   II. Title
BF697.P67   158'.1   76-53340
ISBN: 0-89087-141-8

1 2   3   4   5   6   7   8   9   10   —   82   81   80   79   78   77

Contents

To My Dear Parents in Israel
Lisa and Zonia Kritzman
With All My Love

להורי היקרים בישראל
ליזה וזוניה קריצמן
באהבה עמוקה

Introduction

Why do these words sound contradictory? Chances are, you are wondering how a "negative" trait like selfishness can be made positive in any setting other than the jungle! Certainly, you would be hurt if someone told you that you were selfish. And yet . . . the cultivation of selfishness is necessary for your happiness.

Most of us are raised to think only of the negative aspects of "being selfish"—and of those there are plenty. Being selfish usually means being self-centered to the extent that you lack concern for others. It often implies that you are haughty, obstinate, and over-bearing. It is generally a way of saying that you are being childish. And of course, most of us would agree that these are traits we wish to avoid—if only so that we can feel good about ourselves. Your problem *may* be that you go to such lengths to avoid the "sin" of selfishness, that you deny yourself the love and respect you deserve!

Positive selfishness is a sign of mental health. You need a certain amount of selfishness in order to defend yourself against the selfishness of others. You need the courage to say "No" to people or situations that would exploit you or diminish you. You require the self-love and self-esteem to allow you to know that your needs deserve to be tended to. Your life, happiness, and health are your responsibil-

1

ity, and no one will see to them but you. A constructively selfish person recognizes this and actively works to live, change, and improve life!

The development of positive selfishness comes through self-awareness, self-acceptance, self-esteem, and self-assertiveness. Positive selfishness helps you to be a doer, one who does not simply dream, hesitate, or continually complain that life is unfair. It recognizes that you are the creator of your happiness, the possessor of a self-loving and self-respecting attitude.

Can you achieve this? You can if you want to.

Do you want to? You do if you love yourself.

If you are bored, unhappy, or discontented, do you love yourself enough to want to be happier? If you do, this book will show you how you can improve the four areas of your life upon which positive selfishness is based. If you don't love yourself enough to even *want* to change, this book is *definitely* for you. It will help you develop the positive attitude you need to initiate change.

1. Are you *aware* of your feelings, needs, and moods at all times? You can learn awareness skills. They are simple and exciting—and effective!

2. Are you capable of *accepting* yourself the way you are, and not measuring yourself by others' standards? You can learn self-acceptance skills!

3. Do you have high *self-esteem*? Without a good self-image and high self-esteem, you cannot become an assertive individual.

4. Can you *assert* yourself, without fear or guilt? Without assertiveness skills, you cannot be a positively selfish individual.

"Positive selfish behavior" is the total sum of these four characteristics. Awareness builds acceptance, which is the basis for self-esteem. Self-esteem allows you to develop self-assertiveness, which is the basis for the practice of positive selfishness.

The process of developing self-awareness, -acceptance, -esteem, and assertiveness is a process of personal growth. As we guide you into this process, we will ask you to reflect upon yourself, and to take concrete actions leading towards change. As you will see, some of our exercises will be "intellectual," and others will be "practical." Personal change has both inner and outer components (emotion and action), and you must deal with both.

As a starting point, let's briefly discuss various feelings—positive, and especially negative—people have about themselves. You will learn new ways of dealing with these feelings. We all have feelings of anger, loneliness, anxiety, low self-esteem, and meaninglessness at times—but not all of us accept these feelings. Most of us are frightened by such "negative" feelings, and try to banish them from our lives. We often attempt to will ourselves to be "good"—and we define goodness as comprised of an impossible collage of socially endorsed qualities and completely devoid of the entire range of very human "negative" emotions. The first step towards self-esteem, then, is to develop an awareness of your total emotional range and accept this as your full humanity. Allow yourself to feel all of the universal human feelings. In this way you discover what you are—without quivering in the face of what you were taught you "should be."

One of the major difficulties you may encounter when you undertake a program of personal growth is the false expectation that you will become something other than yourself. Such a goal negates your own existence and your ability to accept your *self*. It denies you the ability to relax and say, "Where I am and what I am is beautiful, and I like it." False expectations about personal growth generate internal friction, instead of tranquility. You may put a lot of energy into an effort to "measure up" to a standard alien to your own being.

We prefer to emphasize personal authenticity and indi-

vidual uniqueness—and encourage you to find fulfillment
by building confidence in your own unique qualities and
abilities. This is truly freedom for the inner self: "The freedom to be me."

The development of self-awareness, self-acceptance and
self-esteem is not totally a lonely process. True, we must
learn to communicate with ourselves, but we also must
relate to others. This is an undeniable element in personal
happiness. We will discuss means by which you can improve your ability to communicate with friends, family,
and lovers—methods for the improvement of communication skills, techniques for recognizing and asserting your
own needs, and guidelines on how to listen and respond
to others as they do the same.

When we deal with the question of life's meaning, we
ask you to recognize your personal responsibility in life.
We cannot offer you a list of things from which you can
choose in order to have a meaningful life. Each human
being is unique, and what is meaningful to each of us
varies as we do. What we will discuss are methods of
value clarification, setting goals for yourself, and the development of will—the skills which enable you to discover
and put meaning into your life.

Finally, we would warn you about abusive approaches
to personal growth. There are many popular approaches
to "growth" which are ultimately counterproductive because of the intimidation and regimentation they involve.
Beware, whenever a book or a friend provides you with a
slick "growth formula," and then implies that if you don't
accept this method there is something wrong with you, or
you are a "hopeless case." This is coercive and conformist.
True growth is free and self-expressive. Do not let yourself
get lost in the interests of seeming "in" or "hip." Affirm
your *self*. Protect yourself. It's positively selfish to do so.

chapter 1

The Roots of Self-Esteem

You are the tree, the roots, the trunk, the branches, leaves, blossoms, and fruit. Your self-esteem is developed through a nurturing environment. The sources of nutrience are the soil in which you, the tree, are growing. The nurturing soil is your parents: they touched you from the day you were born, the many hugs and strokes you received, their loving and accepting expressions, their verbal and nonverbal expressions of encouragement, acceptance, love, tenderness—all of the many messages you got as a growing child that you were welcome in their life, that you are special and beautiful and good just the way you are. Their "strong" message was that you didn't have to live up to any expectation but just *be*. You didn't have to become anything you are not.

Some don't get this vital nourishment from a loving family. The roots of such a child are not as strong and stable. This child learns not to trust, not to share, not to hope, not to *be*. When we grow with such insecurities, we learn to rely on ourselves, our friends, our lovers, our spouse, our children. For some, work, accomplishments, creative product are the roots of self-esteem. For others, their appearance, their looks, the clothes they wear, the house they live in or the car they drive are enough.

All these are the roots of self-esteem. No one has the

right to determine which are more nourishing or needed. You can only choose for yourself.

Self-esteem grows through an inner feeling of positive self-concept and self-acceptance. Equally, a support system is essential for building self-esteem. In the past the family was an important source of the support system. The family unit was stable and secure. A person could always rely on his large family's support. If a parent was not available there was always someone else to go to.

Today, families are not providing the same source of security. The family is mobile and therefore the roots are not deep, neither geographically nor emotionally. Work which gave gratification in seeing a finished product has also lost its simplistic significance. Many people who are employed by large organizations are part of a large team and their individual contribution is not acknowledged with credit which can enhance self-esteem. As support systems become unstable and unreliable, people are looking for groups to which they can belong and identify.

Myth and Reality About Self-Esteem

MYTH 1: The Perfect Happiness. This myth promises that if you have self-esteem, you will be happy all the time, that life will be a pain-free paradise. It is essential to know that pain, anger, and sadness are part of life experiences and are unavoidable parts of happiness. A person with high self-esteem can take higher risk and admit the vast range of his feelings. He is willing to experience his feelings and is not afraid of them.

MYTH 2: The Total Transformation. A person who looks for the total, instant change in the way he feels about himself, cannot accept small changes. In order to build self-esteem we have to be aware of small changes and gain strength and a positive self-image about ourselves from the small accomplishments.

MYTH 3: Somebody Else Will Do It for Me. Outside sources are valuable in aiding a person to build self-esteem. However, you cannot rely on others to do it for you. Such a dependency makes you vulnerable; you do the things you do for others in order to receive an exchange of acceptance and praise, you are dependent on other's evaluation of your worth. Under such conditions self-esteem cannot have healthy roots.

MYTH 4: Verbal Reassurance. Verbal praise is valued only as much as the source's credibility. If you don't trust the person who tries to reassure you, you might become suspicious and distrustful. In such cases verbal reassurance can be negative. Only when it is specific, appropriate, and personal, to the person and for the occasion, can it be positive and reassuring. The pleasure that the giver gets out of giving you compliments shows he cares about you and is involved with you—this is an important factor in the building of self-esteem.

MYTH 5: Self-Disclosure Is Dangerous to Self-Esteem. By sharing yourself you take many risks of being hurt. We do take risks; we grow through taking risks. This is the only way to learn to trust. The disclosure game can be very negative if you want to impress your partner with all the positive aspects of you. The main reason people are afraid to express negative feelings is the fear of rejection. What stops many from being open and honest is the thought that "you will not like me, you will never know who I really am but only who *I want you to think* I am. Don't get close to me. I will never dare getting close to anyone." In building self-esteem we learn to dare and take risks and disclose our true selves. The rewards of finding that people really like you for *who you are* is a tremendous reward and is worth the risk.

SELF-DISCLOSURE

1. What are the four fears you have in disclosing yourself to others?
2. What are the four hopes you have about his/her response after you have disclosed yourself?
3. What is the one thing you will never tell about yourself?
4. What is the one thing you are proud to tell about yourself?
5. Expand the list (question 4), add ten things you like about yourself.
6. Which parts of yourself have you expressed up to now and which parts of yourself would you like to express?

Your choices now are not better than those in the past. Nor is it too late to express your*self* now because you are too old or too ___ or too ___. You can do it, and by feeling and thinking positively you will feel better about yourself.

Practice self-disclosure with one person (partner, friend, or stranger), take three risks. Don't take a risk which will create anxiety or one which you will regret sharing. Yet, take a risk that under other conditions you would choose *not* to share with anybody.

The roots of self-esteem are a beginning of life process. A process of being *aware* of self, *knowing* yourself, *liking* yourself each day a little better:
   —accepting yourself the way you are;
   —accepting yourself the way you want to be;
   —changing yourself in a positive direction, the way you are able to like the changing self even more;

—accepting your positive self-image, your body, the way you look, the way you move, the way you dress, walk, dance, talk, laugh, and cry. Your body is a statement of the choices you make today about your life! Respect your body and your life—and your choices;

—being *positively selfish*, liking yourself equally and more than anybody else, feeling that you are very special for yourself.

—respecting your time. Time is life; by having control over time you can improve the quality of your life and improve your self-esteem;

—indulge yourself in pleasure and give yourself permission to *be*; it is your responsibility alone to make yourself happy;

—don't expect anyone to build your self-esteem for you, you are the only one committed to yourself;

—learn how to make decisions and assert yourself. You are the summation of your decisions; you are responsible to yourself to see them through.

Ten Roots in Building Self-Esteem

1. The process of building self-esteem is active and continuous all your life.
2. You are the only one to *give it to yourself*. Remember: If somebody else can "give it" to you, he can just as easily "take it away" from you.
3. Clarify the values and priorities for your life. What is important and desirable for you? Are you living in accord with your priorities?
4. You have to give up something to gain something else—which is more important to you now? Decisions are trade-offs: You may be lonely in order to express your need to be creative; you may give up friends in order to have more privacy. Be aware of the *price* you are ready to pay for trade-offs.
5. Listen to the different parts of yourself. Often they are

in conflict, they push you in different directions. You have to choose, in each conflict, to which part of yourself you will respond. If you don't make an assertive choice you stay in stagnation.

6. Give up your images—who you are—of the past. As a summation of your early life experiences you may feel unlovable, stupid, lazy, fat, ugly, always late, etc. In reality, you may be really thin at present and yet in your image you see yourself fat as you were in the past. Reequate your self-image with who you are today.

7. Think positively about yourself. Substitute positive adjectives for negative ones and reassure yourself that you deserve what you get and you will give yourself more of what you want: "I am lovable, I deserve to be loved, and I will allow myself to accept love, I will also allow others to love me."

8. You are committed to give yourself a gift. Every day you will give yourself at least one thing that makes you feel better about yourself. Establish what these things are to be and be consistent in this commitment.

9. It is up to you, and only you, to make yourself happy and make yourself love yourself. Try all the exercises in this book more than once and then create your own. Ask yourself: Is there a new way, or a better way to like myself today? Don't give up trying, experimenting. Being discouraged, frustrated, sad, low, are all part of growing and changing. Learning to love somebody (yourself), after many years of loving very little or not at all, takes effort and sometimes pain.

10. Breakthrough; redefining and resynthesizing take time, a breakthrough will not happen instantly. Allow time for the process to work and enjoy small achievements, appreciate small changes. When you feel very good about yourself one day and then the next day bad again, don't give up. This is the way it is. If you

like yourself just a little more each day, enjoy it! When you feel alive and open to the world you will get your reward from others too. Don't be dependent on others, yet accept the mutual sharing.

The more you give yourself self-esteem, the more you are able to share with others, the more others will share with you.

chapter 2

The Starting Point: Affirm Your Feelings

Feelings

Feelings are inescapable. Running the gamut from joy to utter despair, they are the warp and woof in the fabric of our lives. We cater to them, are motivated by them, and yet, most people lack even a basic awareness of their own feelings.

One must be aware of ones feelings before he can cope with them effectively. This is a difficult task—because in childhood, people are not taught to explore their own feelings and preferences, but are instead expected to mirror those of their parents. In addition, children are generally admonished to repress whole areas of "unacceptable" feelings—such as anger, hostility, sometimes even spontaneity. In view of this, it is not surprising to encounter an adult who has difficulty telling you what, or how, he feels.

As you might expect, this problem is far more extensive in men than in women. During childhood, little girls are allowed to express feelings (except aggressiveness) much more openly than are little boys. Traditionally, boys have been socialized to mask feelings of fear and tenderness in favor of the "masculine" feelings of confidence, assertiveness, and ambition. The product of this is evident in almost every counseling group. The most common complaint wives have about husbands is their apparent inability to "share feelings." The men generally express as their greatest complaint the fact that their wives are "always pressing to know how I feel about something."

So, first of all, we have to become aware of our feelings—which is no simple task—and an especially difficult undertaking for men, who have to overcome the additional barrier of social stereotypes regarding "masculine" feelings and behavior.

A person who is in search of happiness and inner peace is in search of self. This is not an intellectual task—that is, it cannot ever be accomplished by the intellect alone. Stop for a moment and contemplate happiness—or dissatisfaction. These are states of being which are defined by feeling, and as such, are indivisible from emotion. True, you can rationally analyze your feelings and your life situation—but you must not lose track of the fact that you cannot reduce these to decision issues, devoid of feeling. The decision, the "answer," to most problems can be found by asking yourself, "How do I feel about it?" If in the past you systematically attempted to deal with all things intellectually, then perhaps the easiest way for you to begin to change is to make the decision that you will allow feelings a role in your life. You must get used to the idea that emotion is part of the whole, just as intellect is part of the whole. You must commit yourself to giving space to your feelings, and allow yourself to experience them.

Ah, you say, "But I don't know how I feel about most things!" You are not alone. The main thing is to have the courage and the commitment to learn how you feel. You can do this, because the feelings *are* there. It's just that after years of repression and denial, you've lost the knack for recognizing them.

Developing an Awareness of Your Feelings

Find a place—a room or a setting—where you have solitude. Make yourself comfortable—recline or sit, and adjust your body and limbs so that you feel relaxed. Make sure there are no tense areas in your body—check to make certain your palms are open, not clenched, your back feels supple, your neck is not held stiffly.

Now, locate the sensation of "your inner core." To do this, close your eyes and take several deep breaths. You will probably sense a direction towards which your inner self gravitates. Is this direction up or down? Is it towards a specific bodily organ? (Some people say they have a sense of "center" in their stomach; some, in their chest; others, in their head; and so on.) Relax and try to focus on the experience of slipping in the direction of your "inner core." Can you describe this "center" you approach? Is it hot or cold? Is it slippery? Is it open? Some people sense that their "inner core" is a dark place; others, that it is bright. What you visualize is a very individual thing.

If after several attempts you have difficulty visualizing the location of your "inner core," then simply say to yourself, "Here I am, at a place where all truths about me are known, all my inner fears laid bare, and all emotions run free."

Now list eight feelings which touch your core most intensely. We all experience 'good' and 'bad' (pleasant and unpleasant) feelings, so seek out the three or four pleasant feelings which evoke the most intense response from your inner self, and also the three or four most unpleasant feelings. If these feelings don't come readily to mind, you might ponder each of the feelings on the following list and see which evoke the greatest response in you:

jealousy	fear of exposure	joy
envy	low self-esteem	security, safety
hate	loneliness	nurturing
fear of unknown	fear of weakness	peace
guilt	love	triumph
anxiety	loyalty	pride in accomplishment
fear of failure	trust	enthusiasm,

Whatever eight feelings you put on your list, write them down! We will call this list your "doors to your inner self." Now you know eight of the most intense feelings you have, and you have labelled them. Your next task is to become acquainted with them. Which of these feelings are you most ashamed of? Which do you most wish to experience? Which can you share—that is, disclose to others? If you can't share a particular feeling, why?

One by one, take each of your "doors" and relive the feelings you have in association with it. Recall experiences you have had—perhaps even in childhood—which make the feeling so intense for you. Make notes for future reference. (For example, you might note that you feel deeply a sense of worthlessness, and that you can recall this feeling in childhood in connection with family remarks that you were not a planned child, but an "unfortunate mistake." You might note that you remember crying in your bed at night, hoping that your parents wouldn't decide to give you away if you didn't behave.) This is not a happy task, recalling experiences connected with unpleasant experiences; but it is extremely important. These "doors" will become your reference points when dealing with all other tensions and fears you encounter, and in understanding your motivations and ideals. Even when you feel numb, and can't come in contact with your present feelings, you will be able to look back over this list and these notes and say to yourself, "I know I have feelings, for these are feelings which affected me very powerfully at one time, and which probably are connected to my sense of numbness today."

Becoming Aware of Your Feelings Through Your Body

Another way of getting in touch with your feelings is by becoming more aware of your body. Your body is pretty objective, so focus on the signals it gives you, because it is continually responding to situations. Pay attention to how your body reacts when you are in different situations. How do you feel when you meet new people—are you tense, are you relaxed? What does your stomach do when you are in an argument with someone? Do you find your hands clenched when you have been thinking about certain topics? Attend to these bodily signals, and respond to them!

Some people are so cut off from their feelings they actually resist attending to their body's signals. In such a case, I try to put them in a very awkward situation—for example, I might ask them to stand up on the table and sing. This produces all kinds of inescapable body signals, and we start from there. This same person often has difficulty relating bodily reactions—shakey legs, headaches, sweaty palms, etc.—to emotions.

The Mind-Body Connection

Are you aware of tensions in your entire body and able to recognize when any portion of your body is not relaxed? Many of us are tense so much of the time, it feels "normal" to us. So, begin by teaching yourself the sensation of relaxation. Beginning with your neck, tense it and hold it tense for thirty seconds. Then, release the muscles, sigh deeply, and sense the pleasure of tension fading into looseness and relaxation. Repeat this pattern of tensing muscles and then relaxing them, working through your entire body: arms, hands, stomach, legs, ankles, and so on. Do this very slowly, and take the time necessary to tune in to the sensations of relaxation and tenseness. If you will do this twice a day for two weeks, you will become well attuned to detecting tension in your musculature.

As a next step, work on discerning the connections between your bodily tensions and your psychological being. When you discover your palms clenched, for example, say to yourself, "I know there is a connection between my palms and my psyche: what is it?" Review each of the emotional "doors" you have identified, and see if you can find a connection. When you find the connection, deal with the emotion involved. Face it, and expose it. For example, you might find that whenever you experience a tense, sour stomach, you are also fearing failure.

Awareness of these connections makes it possible to prevent physiological reactions to feelings. If, for example, you come to know that you suffer indigestion whenever you have to entertain your husband's business associates, you can then take steps to deal with your trepidations about entertaining—and prevent indigestion.

In addition, there is another payoff connected with the identification of bodily tension. Just as psychological states feed into your physical being and help create muscular tension, so the release of muscular tension can help ease psychological strain. If you are feeling vaguely anxious and note that your legs are tense and tightly crossed, for example, uncross and relax your legs as you take three deep breaths. You will probably find that this has a temporary effect in diminishing your overall anxiety.

How do you express an emotion that is important? When you hit on an emotion, repeat it several times, each time with greater volume. You'll be surprised at the effect!

So many times I have seen people say, tremblingly, "I feel scared. . . ." I ask them to repeat it several times, and amazingly, it is transformed: "I AM SCARED, SCARED, SCARED!" Usually, a whole string of related feelings rush out, triggered by the expression of the fear. All kinds of feelings that you haven't allowed yourself to experience can be brought out in this way. As you experiment with this, you will notice there are certain kinds of feelings you do not want to accept in yourself. You have an internal censor, which tries to hold back feelings that are dangerous to your self-image or to your feeling of security. You are going to have to give yourself permission to be aware of these feelings, and to express them as well.

FACING NEGATIVE FEELINGS

Ask yourself, "Why do I resist dealing with negative feelings?" Are you ashamed of them? Do you feel that they will overcome you? Or are they just too painful for you to relive and reexamine? If they are too painful, just skip them for the time being. *But* you must make a note to yourself, "I am not yet ready to deal with my negative feelings (e.g., jealousy, guilt, fear of failure, anxiety), but *I have them.*"

As the weeks pass, ask yourself periodically, "Am I ready to examine one of my unpleasant feelings now?" Eventually, you will be able to explore these feelings, too. The main thing is not to let yourself brush them aside and pretend they are not there and affect your present motivations, responses and experiences.

When you do deal with negative feelings—e.g., anger—try to make yourself aware of the risks you perceive as being connected with it. Example: If you have anger, and this causes you to be fearful, ask yourself, "What is so awful about my anger? What do I risk by disclosing it to someone, or by expressing it?" Only in this way can you become fully aware of your total self—the negative as well as the positive.

The Validity of Feelings

Even when people become aware of their feelings, they often do not accord them any validity. Some people have a tendency to reject emotion as being extraneous because it is not rational. I would suggest that this is "the rationality trap," a syndrome of our era. It is the product of a scientific, technological society which emphasizes the necessity to find valid reasons and causes for all phenomena. But when you apply this to the world of emotions, you run into immense difficulty if you conclude that you must have reasons for your feelings in order for them to be valid.

This orientation is one which regards feelings as being suspect—until they are "justified." But one can seldom prove that one has a "right" to a particular feeling. There are always people in similar circumstances who feel and act differently. So, the feeling is suspect. Of course, any person with sensitivity or any amount of insecurity can always look into himself and find some way of blaming himself for his feelings. Does he dislike his neighbor? He concludes that this is proof of his own lack of charity, and that if he were a "good person," he wouldn't feel that way. As a result, he hates himself, and represses the unacceptable feeling.

There is also a corollary to the rationality trap: you accept the fact that feelings have a validity of their own, but you think that feelings, by themselves, can never be a justifiable basis for action. For example, let's say you feel very miserable in your marriage. You accept this feeling, and at the same time you think, "I don't have any good reasons for leaving my marriage. Yes, I'm miserable, but that's no reason. . . ." This distrust of feelings is a distrust of listening to your inner self.

Many people get angry at themselves because they have feelings! We have a tendency to consider a certain class of feelings to be "weaknesses." Of course, the entire range of positive feelings—affection, joy, love, creativity, enthusiasm—are all acceptable. But the "negative" feelings are threatening, and we try to banish them—fear, anxiety, hostility, anger, depression, and so on. Somehow, when you feel these things, you tend to regard them as danger signals—signals that you are not "together," that things are not as they "should be" within you, that you are "weak." For example, anxiety often causes greater anxiety, because it is interpreted as a sign of "losing control." These fears may be reinforced by unrealistic ideas about how other people feel on a daily basis. We assume that other people are able to handle things calmly, in stride, happily—that they are not anxious and depressed as we periodically are. We assume that the fully developed, mature person is happy, fulfilled, calm, and in control. Insofar as we aspire to be this way, we see our own feelings as betraying our shortcomings.

One problem with feelings is related to common misperceptions about "maturity." Somehow, many people seem to equate childhood with irrationality, emotionality, and spontaneous feelings. We also accept certain behaviors in children on the basis that "they are not adult." Therefore, there is a tendency to assume that progress towards adulthood is made by the repression of emotion and spontaneity, and by replacing these with rationality, intellect, and control. As a result, many people feel that in order to be an adult, they have to deny their fears, anxieties, enthusiasms, and even their joy. We have to accept the fact that the whole person contains both sets of characteristics, quite naturally. And both "parts" have to be accepted and nourished. Allow "irrational" feelings to exist. Experience and express them.

Conflicting and Changing Feelings

As mature adults, we have full capabilities and responsibilities, but we also retain the honest, central part of ourselves—the childlike flow of feeling. When feelings are allowed to flow, you can then experience them. If, for example, you discern an inner anger, let yourself feel it and release it. Expressing a feeling doesn't necessarily mean expressing it to another person—you might punch a pillow, or shout in an empty room.

Expression of feeling can also be a verbal undertaking, and for this, the "empty chair dialogue" developed by Fritz Perls, a founder of Gestalt Therapy, is very helpful. Sit down in one chair, and face an empty chair. The empty chair is the feeling you want to deal with. Tell the empty chair how you feel about it. Then, when you sense the feeling fighting back, *move* and sit in the other chair and speak out that point of view. By "talking to the feeling" you will discover how extensive it is, and what it (you) needs.

As you develop awareness of feelings, and the ability to express them, you may discover that you have conflicting feelings. Many people allow this to throw them into despair or paralyzing frustration, asking, "How do I know which of these feelings represents the *real me?*" There is a fallacy here—the unfounded assumption that one of the feelings is genuine, and the other "false." In fact, both feelings are genuine, and you are not unusual for being "inconsistent." So you have conflicting emotions, and the best course of action is to have a dialogue with both, or all, of them. You assign a chair to each feeling, and then move from chair to chair as you speak (out loud) from each "emotional viewpoint." Don't expect one feeling to emerge the victor! In most cases, the dialogue results in an agreement among the conflicted feelings, generally some sort of compromise in which each emotion is respected, although not all get what they want.

Another problem is a fear of changing your feelings. Many people feel guilty, or doubt themselves, when they discover that their feelings about something, or someone, have changed. This is what I call the "consistency trap." You cannot assume that your feelings are, or ever will be, static. You are a dynamic system. You live in a world that changes, and you will change. If you discover your feelings have altered, this is not a sign that something is wrong with you; in fact, it is probably a sign you are healthy and growing. Let changing feelings occur. Use your awareness of them as an opportunity for creative adjustment in your life.

Far too many people have a tyrant within themselves that commands them to change their feelings! This tyrant is a torturer, because you cannot change your feelings on command—not even when you wish you could. The command comes from a person's inner censor, which disallows some feelings, and requires others. For example, you might think, "I should love my father," although you do not. These "shoulds" originate from an inner sense that tells you this is something you must feel or do in order to be loved. Self-esteem is at the base of this problem—it should not be dependent on manufacturing feelings that aren't spontaneous. If you can love yourself and respect yourself for what you are, then you are not dependent on this unspoken promise: "If only I feel this, then I'll be acceptable." You *are* acceptable, just as you are.

Some people attempt to resolve the inadequate self-concept which results from these "shoulds" by pretending. They feel, for example, "I do not love my mother, although I should love my mother. Since I don't love Mother as I should, I am a bad person. My absence of love proves that I am unworthy. But I will pretend that I love her, and this will compensate for my unworthiness." This is a tragic path to take, because it means living by lying to yourself. Will this help you? No. One day you will admit,

"I am a fake." It is far better to accept the fact that you do not love your parent. Then behave in whatever way you think is best, within the range of what your emotions will allow.

Anxiety and Failure

When people seek counseling because they need help in dealing with their feelings, they are usually concerned with the negative emotions. Anxiety and the fear of failure are at the top of the list of tormentors, and have to be faced before the person can begin to grow into a more fulfilled being.

To be anxious is to distrust the world. Most anxieties reduce to this common theme: fear of a threatening world which is ready to destroy you in unpredictable ways.

Anxious people generally feel helpless, and dependent upon the actions and judgments of others. Simultaneously, they strive very hard to be in control at all times. As an example of a simple case of anxiety, consider the woman who is giving a dinner party for her husband's associates. She is terribly anxious, lest her party be a failure, because this would, she assumes, make her a failure in the eyes of others. In fact, she assumes that her guests will sneer at her behind her back if any little thing goes wrong. As a result, she attempts to *control* the situation by working to be absolutely perfect, and thereby protect herself from others. Every aspect of the party is planned in minute detail, and she expends massive amounts of energy reviewing all plans in her mind, over and over again. In this example, you can see all the elements of anxiety: dependence on the judgments of others, the assumption that "they" will judge you harshly if you do not "measure up," the need for help in facing the threat, the attempt to be in total control in order to stave off anxiety feelings.

Since anxious persons strive for control as a means of coping with fear, they are apt to suffer torment whenever faced with unknown situations—for the unknown is by definition unpredictable, and therefore is beyond sure control. Hence, anxiety blocks personal growth by shutting off the individual's willingness to experiment and try new things.

DEMONSTRATE THAT YOU CAN CONQUER ANXIETY

Are you ashamed to admit your anxieties? If so, you have lots of company. It's quite normal to feel that you alone suffer anxious moments—but it is not true! If you can drop the sense of shame and secretiveness surrounding your anxieties, it will be much easier to confront the fear and distrust on which they are based. Anxieties are not permanent; they can be overcome with a little work.

You have within you the resources to overcome your anxieties. To be able to use these resources just takes a little practice. As with all things, it's easiest to begin with a small step and use this for building confidence. First, make a list of all the things that cause you anxiety. Then when you have a range of anxieties, examine them and pick one which is relatively concrete and amenable to an incremental strategy. For example, let's assume you have anxieties about being in a crowded room, about dying, about failing at work, and about flying in an airplane. You might begin with your fear of crowded rooms, as this is the most concrete fear, and one which you can deal with in gradual steps.

First, examine this anxiety. Make a list, in which you try to identify all the reasons why you are anxious in such a situation. You may discover that you are really afraid that you will feel sick, and won't be able to get through the crowd to the exit, or that you think you will have to go to the bathroom and won't be able to find it.

Construct a plan. Once you have identified the specific fears which underlie your anxiety, construct a plan of action. In our example, you might decide, "If I go into a crowded room, like a restaurant, I will sit near the door. That way, I will know that I can get up and leave if I want to."

Implement your plan. When you make a dinner reservation, make it clear that you must have a table by the door. Enlist the cooperation of your spouse, lover, or a good friend as a dinner companion—someone who understands the significance of what you are attempting and will not interfere. When the time comes, do not hesitate to use your pre-planned "escape route" as often as you need to. If you feel anxiety coming on, get up and leave for a few moments. When you see how easy it is to leave, you will find it possible to come back.

Practice! Go into a restaurant in this way several times. Eventually you will find that you have practiced enough to convince yourself that you dare to sit a few tables further from the door. When this time comes, do it, and congratulate yourself! Little by little, you will see yourself overcoming your anxiety.

Triumph over even a minor anxiety will show you that you have the skills and resources to tackle and overcome larger anxieties. This builds your confidence, and confidence is the ultimate destroyer of anxiety.

Obviously, anxiety is connected to a very low sense of self-esteem. This may sound paradoxical if you happen to know that particular type of anxious person who gives wonderful parties, excells in school, or "works miracles" in his profession. To the observer, this person appears to have very high self-esteem because of his high achievements. Underneath, however, he is very unsure of his personal worth. He feels he must "measure up" to the very exacting standards he sets for himself in order to be "acceptable" to the world.

Some people are motivated by fear—fear of failure.

They feel that if they do not measure up, they will be snuffed out, literally extinguished! And so, striving and excelling are life-or-death propositions for them. Failure itself can be so threatening that a person tries to "control" failure by never endeavoring. If you refuse to try anything, you cannot fail. (On the other hand, many overachieving children may refuse to try new things because they fear success! In their tortured world, success in a new pursuit simply means an added burden to carry— something additional which they must "live up to" time and time again.) The anxious over-achiever tends to see the world in terms of black and white. That is, he either wins or loses, passes or fails, lives or dies. He has no sense of the middle ground, in which a person is somewhat successful, relatively meritorious, or sufficiently capable. He feels he must "meet the standard" or fail. And the "standard" is ultimate perfection. Since this is an unrealistic standard, his fear of failure is a very realistic fear.

REASSESSING YOUR FEARS OF FAILURE

Failure and fears of failure are most generally related to a fear of making mistakes. So ask yourself, "Why am I so afraid to make mistakes?" and "What can happen to me if I make a mistake?" Many people feel that if they make mistakes, they show that they are stupid, incompetent, unworthy of love, and so on. If you feel this way you should begin by rethinking your view of mistakes. Mistakes are positive contributions to your growth as a person. There can be no personal development without mistakes to learn by. Admitting and sharing mistakes makes you close to others. Fear of disclosing one's mistakes is based on deep insecurity, not on "superior standards."

The desire to make *no* mistakes is really a desire to be perfect—and superior to everyone else! Why should you be free of error when it is the human condition to err, to blunder, and then to do one's best to right things? So, accept the fact that making mistakes makes you human. It has been said that, "The ideal to be a perfect person is the ideal of a perfect ass."

List all the things you've done that you consider mistakes and failures. Then note next to each one: did you admit to yourself at the time it happened that it was a mistake/failure (or did you deny it)? Could you share it with someone (disclose it)? If not, why?

For each mistake, make a plan of action for avoiding a repetition of the mistake. But a word of caution—don't make grandiose plans which demand perfection, or performance so superior that it destines you to repeated failures. Make plans for improvements, not for grand transformations!

Carry out your plan for avoiding repetition of a specific mistake. If it works, congratulate yourself. If it does not work, DON'T castigate yourself for failing! Give yourself permission to learn and be experimental by saying to yourself, "Well, I'm one step towards solving this problem. At least I've tried this scheme and found that it doesn't work. . .so, on to another approach!" You can do it, if you are persistent.

Once you have found a method for avoiding a given mistake, be very self-conscious about applying it again and again. But don't require yourself never to slip. After all, each situation is new and different, and one solution may not work on every occasion. Again, that's part of being human. Just take it in stride and keep on practicing. After a while, practice makes skill (not perfect).

Guilt

Guilt is probably the most self-destructive of all human emotions. It destroys self-esteem, blocks growth, and in-

flicts great pain. Ironically, it is also a common motivation
behind high personal achievement. Guilt is found wherever the "shoulds" and "oughts" exist, for it arises from
the sense that you are not fulfilling your responsibilities in
life.

Certainly we all feel guilty upon occasion, and rightfully
so. Perhaps you leave the water running and as a result
the bathroom floor floods. You have necessitated the ex-
pense and trouble of fixing the floor, you know you are
responsible, and you feel guilty. Such instances of guilt
appear and recede from our lives, and although they cause
us discomfort, they are normal and the guilt is real. Many
people, however, suffer undue guilt from unreal causes,
and this is what I call the "guilty person syndrome."

The guilty person imposes guilt upon himself by assuming responsibility for everything that happens to those
around him. He also assumes responsibility for the happiness of those around him, let's say for his spouse or family. With this "because of me" orientation, he perceives
himself to be at fault for every unhappy event or miserable
mood in the household. Kathy is just this sort of person,
for she suffers immense guilt every time Ron, her husband, is unhappy with his work. Ron tries carefully to
explain that it is his job which is the cause of his mood;
Kathy insists that she is at fault "because I ought to be able
to lift his mood and make him happy." Since she cannot
do this, she feels guilty because, as she sees it, her failure
causes Ron to continue suffering!

Basically, the guilty person is one who has low self-
esteem and suffers from feelings of worthlessness. The
guilt is tied to the self-judgment that you are not good
enough—because if you were good enough you could
prevent the unhappiness of others. I have often heard
people express the wish, "If only I could be different, I
could make so-and-so happy." This is the unending put-
down that the guilty person works on himself. Unending,

because this person demands of himself impossible things.

Paradoxical as it may sound, for many people guilt is increased by personal happiness! Kathy is such a person. She does not work and is very happy with her life of children and volunteer work. This intensifies her feeling of guilt towards Ron, because she asks herself, "How can I be happy when Ron suffers so?" She feels guilty that she isn't equally miserable—until finally her spiraling sense of guilt brings her to a state of utter anguish.

What causes a person to assume such unrealistic responsibilities? It generally comes from early childhood, from hearing repeatedly that you are a bad child. Parents create this situation when children are blamed for the parents' own moods or shortcomings. If a mother doesn't feel good, she should take responsibility for her own mood. But if she blames her child, "I'm unhappy and it's your fault," and she follows this pattern repeatedly over the years, the child will come to feel that he is basically responsible for the moods of those around him.

People who feel such responsibility and guilt may also have repressed anger. The child who feels unloved must feel some anger at his parents for depriving him of the affection he needs so much. However, he fears that if he expresses his anger towards them, he will foreclose all possibility of receiving their love. So he chokes back his anger, and after a time, the repression of anger becomes so automatic that he is totally unaware of its existence at the depths of his being. Instead, he is aware only of the anxieties and depressions that stalk him through life.

Guilt and failure and the assumption of power are intimately interconnected. If you feel responsible for everything, then in some unconscious way you believe that you should be able to control the world around you. "If I am better, then others will be happy." What a power! So when everyone isn't happy, you feel you've not only

failed them, you've also failed yourself. Let's assume that
you feel your parents will be happy (or will love you) if
only you get perfect grades. So you work hard and get
wonderful grades—and they still aren't happy (or don't
love you). You conclude you are a total failure, and that
you are so unworthy that nothing you do will ever be good
enough to make you deserving of love.

Most people cannot get out of the guilt-and-failure syndrome until they have built self-esteem. Everything is
closely related to self-esteem. You must like yourself, and
acknowledge human limitations. One of the primary
limitations we all have is that we cannot be responsible for
the happiness of others! If someone is depressed and unhappy, it is his responsibility to do something about it, not
yours! You can be kind, and listen, and help out when you
can and want to, but that's all. You can't help from the
framework of assuming that you are responsible for the
other person's happiness.

Another limitation you have to accept is that you cannot
give things you don't have. For example, if someone asks
for your love, and asserts that he would be happy if only
you loved him, and you do not love him, you cannot give
love. You cannot will yourself to have love that isn't there,
and you shouldn't feel guilty because you do not have love
to give. The other person cannot be allowed to condition
his happiness on whether or not you give something. He
is responsible for his own happiness. You are responsible
for yours.

DEALING WITH GUILT

The feeling of guilt is based on the feeling you are not
good enough, that you have done something terrible to
others, or that you are not doing something you committed yourself to do.

Don't commit yourself to do things you really don't

want to do. The feeling of guilt comes largely from the feeling that you are not doing something you are supposed to do. What about the case where you don't want to do something, but feel you should on the basis of a moral or ethical belief? Even here, examine your element of free action: you endorse a moral belief because you think or feel that it is correct, and you want to live by it. So, you may conclude that you are going to do certain things because they are required by your religion, ethics or whatever—not because they are 'fun' or easy, but because in doing them you satisfy yourself. In this way, even obligatory behavior can become a form of self-assertion and positive selfishness.

Write down all the things that make you feel guilty. Include all of the things which have made you feel guilty in the past. Submit each guilt to examination, and classify it by your response to the following questions:

Do you really owe this person what you think you owe him?

Do you really have to change your behavior in order to conform to his expectations?

Is it possible that you can say to yourself, "Well, he has expectations about what I should do, but I really don't think that I have to fulfill them"? (This is the beginning of self-assertion.)

For example, most of use feel guilty towards our parents. They are aging, and they want visits and letters from us. Now let's say you dislike writing letters. There are two possible courses of action open to you: You can say, "I hate to write letters, but I really want to satisfy my parents' longings for contact with me, so I will rearrange my schedule and provide for myself a definite time each week when I just sit down and write to them." Carry out your resolve. In this example, it would mean disciplining yourself to write your parents weekly.

However, implementation might also mean *not* doing

something. If you realize that you are doing something simply because another person will make you feel guilty if you don't, then say to yourself, "I don't want to do this, and I can learn to assert myself and refuse to do it. If I decide I don't have to do it, then I can also learn not to feel guilty."

Learn to say "no" whenever you are asked to do things you really don't want to do. After the first few times, it will become easier. When you say "yes," *mean* it. And when you mean "no," *say* it! And every time you say what you mean, congratulate yourself!

Up to this point, I have been talking about the "guilty person." I want to add a footnote, however, because I feel that there are a few causes of more generalized guilt which are unique to our era and which affect most people.

I have encountered many young couples who suffer undue anxiety and guilt over the well-being of their children. It strikes me that this anxiety is connected with their overwhelming sense of responsibility for the very presence of the child. In the era of the pill, we can systematically prevent conception. Therefore, the child is viewed not as a blessing from God or a happenstance of fate, but as the product of conscious will on the part of the parents. Insofar as they feel they played God in creating this child, parents tend to assume a total responsibility for the happiness of the child. This is reinforced by current sociological and psychological philosophies which stress the importance of nurture, as opposed to nature. Parents today seem to assume that they can condition and shape every feature of their child's personality. Therefore, when a child is shy and unpopular or slow in school, parents automatically feel that *they* failed. While it is admirable for parents to work to do the very best they can, both child and parent will be better off when mother and father can accept—and respect—even the smallest child as a being quite separate from themselves. A child is not an extension of his parents; he is also not a mere extension of their attempts at conditioning.

Another source of generalized guilt is related to the values of our time. One might say that *relativity of values* has been our paramount concern—with intolerance accepted only when it is directed towards intolerance or authoritarianism. If these values are internalized, and one's self-image includes an emphasis on being tolerant and non-authoritarian, interesting psychological problems result. For one thing, endorsement of the absolute relativity of all values makes it very difficult for many people to act positively and live out an ethical existence. To do so implies positive assertion of a set of values, and a positive assertion is often taken to imply the negation of other, alternative values. This raises self-doubt and guilt feelings, because the negation of competing values is unacceptable to the self-image. Confusion results; and as long as this confusion is unresolved, healthy and fulfilling motivation is difficult.

It is also frowned upon today to be authoritarian. As Bruno Bettelheim has effectively argued,* this leads to many family problems. Parents seek to gain consensus from their children for the rules they set. However, children, being children, don't always give consensus. When confronted with a refusal to grant consensus, many parents feel so guilty about "being authoritarian" that they cannot exert any authority at all. The result is total permissiveness, with no rules, no standards, and no guidelines for the child. This makes the child feel very insecure, and behavioral problems develop.

---

*Bettelheim, Bruno, *Obsolete Youth*. San Francisco: San Francisco Press Inc.

Low Self-Esteem

Success and high achievement are not always signals of high self-esteem. Low self-esteem means simply that you have negative judgments of yourself—the conviction or fear that you are worthless, deficient, or unlovable. It is accompanied by a dependence on the opinions of other people; for example, a man may seek material success as a positive reinforcement from the world—an assurance that he is "OK." Women similarly compensate for low self-esteem, often through seeking "successful" husbands, devoting themselves to "good works," or striving to be the "perfect" wife and mother. In this way, excellent behavior can be merely a bribe to the world, a plea for the rewarding message, "You're really good, after all." Unfortunately, such assurances from others are never quite sufficient to dispel the deep inner feelings of unworthiness.

People with low self-esteem are people who have transferred the power of judgment to the external world, to "others," and therefore are dependent upon the opinions and responses of those "others" for affirmations of their worth as individuals.

Low self-esteem is not always apparent to the casual observer. Consider the "successful" man—can we assume that he has high self-esteem? Perhaps he does. But his quest for success could actually be a search for approval, an attempt to prove to others he is worthwhile as a human being. This is not a secure basis for self-esteem, because there is never a point at which he can say, "This is enough." He must keep on being a success (that is, keep on furnishing proof of his worthiness), in order to get external assurances that he is an adequate man. Like a hamster-run, this leads nowhere, for it never leads to any *personal conviction* of worth. No one can provide you with a sense of self-esteem; you must provide it for yourself, because only YOU can settle the issue and decide that you're OK.

I might add that the problem of self-esteem is related to the question of identity. I see many people who are casting about for their identity, asking "Who am I?" People who can focus on what they like about themselves generally suffer less from concerns about identity.

You really don't have to like all of yourself. You are made up of many "subselves," and you might like some of them more than others. But once you really decide that some of your subselves are positive, and you like them, you will be much more secure in knowing who you are. When we talk about the search of self, we're actually talking about many selves: the you who relates with family, the you at work, the you who meets strangers, the you who needs love, the you who is angry and aggressive—all of YOU. As you begin to identify your many subselves, you can discover which of them you like, and which you don't like. For example, you may say, "I really like myself as a mother, and I feel good about me that way, but I don't feel so good about myself as a wife." Once you understand the selves that exist—and how you feel about each of them—you must start building a part of yourself that says, "I really think I'm OK. I like myself, and I'm proud of myself. I'm not what I'd like to be in all areas, but I really do a fine job at_____." This is one way of building self-esteem, a respect for your whole self, while realizing that your subselves run the gamut from strong to weak and from tender to hostile. Self-esteem gives you strength and confidence to continue to grow, to try to change, and to take risks. You know that you are basically lovable, and that other people—some, but not all—will love you because of what you have to offer. Therefore, you wouldn't be demolished if you were without any of the meaningful relationships you have now, because there are more people in the world who could love you and care for you. You're not dependent on just one source of support and affection. Building self-esteem is the central concern in building positive selfishness.

AN OVERVIEW OF YOUR SELF- ESTEEM*

Using your journal, write out the answers to each of the following questions as fully as possible:

1. Are you dependent on the judgments of others? In what areas?

2. How do you view yourself—your appearance, personality, intellect, emotional being, character?

3. How do you think others view you? (Compare to question above.)

4. Do you have a sense of meaning and fulfillment in your life?

5. Do you have close, fulfilling friendships?

Construct a plan of gradual steps you can undertake to improve your general love for yourself. You could consider including the following suggestions.

Seek out honest feedback. Discover whether or not you are judging yourself too harshly, and whether other people actually view you in the way you think they do. Ask only people you trust and respect! It is important that you be able to believe their answers, and know that they are not lying to you when they tell you positive (as well as negative) things about yourself.

---

*Content for this exercise is drawn from Frieda Porat and Karen Myers, *Changing Your Lifestyle*. New York: Lyle Stuart, 1973. New York: Bantam, 1975.

Work on improving ALL human relationships. People with low self-esteem often do not reach out to others, and therefore lack the warm friendships which affirm self-worth. Plan to call your friends, take the initiative in suggesting shared activities, and let others know that you want to share your good times with them.

Improve your physical appearance. If this is a part of yourself about which you have negative judgments, you can improve your appearance by dressing differently, changing your hairstyle, or losing weight. If need be, ask a friend whose appearance you admire to go shopping with you, to help you over your initial timidity in constructing a new image.

Work to increase the sense of meaning and fulfillment in your life through experimenting with different activities. Whether they be mental, physical, or emotional, discover new activities which truly please you. As you are pleased, you will find you have a greater sense of meaning, and you will like yourself more.

On a daily basis, work on your attitude. You can develop greater self-esteem by repeatedly celebrating your existence as a human being, by becoming tolerant of your human failings, and by rejoicing when good things come your way.

Do not allow low self-esteem to convince you that "None of this will do any good." It will! It is difficult to develop self-esteem in one's adult years, and it requires courage. But it can certainly be done. Assess your attitude by writing in your journal each night; as you see the "excuses" for not changing come out, reject them forcefully, for they are remnants of your outdated (low) self-image.

People have difficulty *affirming* themselves, but they are often much more afraid of *accepting* themselves! This may appear to be word-play, but it is a significant differentiation.

Any person who is basically honest senses that he has good and bad, strong and weak aspects. But many people try very hard to deny the weaknesses in themselves. The very idea of self-acceptance implies that you must not deny the weaknesses in yourself, but instead, must acknowledge them. To the person who is afraid of his own weaknesses, this is tantamount to admitting defeat; he views it as bowing down his head and saying "Yes, I'm scared and weak and therefore not perfect." This admission is equated in his mind with a *surrender* to his shortcomings and is extremely frightening. His struggle to confine his shortcomings was his attempt to protect himself from a threatening world. I prefer not to take the "total acceptance" approach. I usually find it counterproductive. The individual is often so weakened by this "acceptance" he must go through a lengthy recuperation before he can begin to grow.

On the other hand, it is much easier to ask someone to affirm himself. This can begin by simply asking him to make positive statements about some of his subselves, or, if he is so wound up in self-hate that he cannot do even this much, I point out—repeatedly—his positive characteristics. As positive statements are repeated, you can begin to develop the idea that you *are* these good things, regardless of other "bad" things that also can be pointed out. This affirmation of the positive self is entirely different from the acceptance of the negative self.

An affirmation is positive and active, and leads you to view your *self* as *the* active factor in your life. Once you have affirmed yourself, you know that you are "good" as a person, and can therefore take responsibility for your own life, including the responsibility to try to change those things which make you unhappy. On the other hand, acceptance connotes receiving, passivity, and a certain bowing to fate. "Fate" is external to the self, and an acceptance of fate can take the form of simply resigning from all personal responsibility for change and improvement in one's own life. These two orientations are so different! The active orientation leads you to take responsibility for your own future—this is the prerequisite for a healthy self.

As you develop self-esteem and an independence from the external judgments of other people, you may suffer pangs of guilt. You aren't alone. Many people who are asserting their own preferences and choices for the first time feel guilty because they are afraid they are being selfish. They are. But in a positive way.

Positive selfishness? Yes! Most of our culture is dominated by the Judeo-Christian ethic, which emphasizes unselfish sacrifice for others, and defines selfishness as immoral. Aren't we all taught that it is better to give than to receive? Don't we quickly learn that we cannot ask for pleasure from others—unless, of course, we "pay" them in some sense? I never deny the existence of negative selfishness, but we shouldn't automatically suffer pangs of guilt and shame whenever we place our own desires first.

Obviously, if you are selfish in a way that is inconsiderate of other people, hurting others, or if you are using and manipulating others—that is *negative* selfishness. Negative because your egocentrism is so extreme that you see others only as tools and objects, whom you don't mind hurting in order to have your own way.

On the other hand, if you assert that you are important, and that you really like yourself and need to please yourself and be happy, then you develop a *positive selfishness*. You see yourself as being responsible for your own needs and happiness. With this attitude you are able to give more of yourself to others and build deeper relationships.

You can communicate effectively with those you love, telling them what you need and encouraging them to tell you of their needs in return. You will also take a great burden off other people! No one likes to feel another is suffering in order to give him happiness. And it is much easier for others to respond to you when they know what you want and how you feel.

Joy and No-Joy

Joy, a key to happiness, is free and available to everyone. The tragic fact is that most people are quite joyless, and are locked into almost constant pessimism and negative attitudes about life. Some seek fun frequently and frantically, but this does little to compensate for the lack of joy. Having fun is almost a social requirement in our culture. We lie, and claim to have had fun when we did not. We spend billions for fun, we organize for fun, and we look foreward to fun things. But in between the games, trips, and cocktail parties, in the moments and hours when we are not being entertained, we sink into listlessness and pessimism. Then we plan another fun event, and live out the week waiting for those few hours when we can "feel alive" again.

People who live like this have never learned how to experience joy. Joy springs from a positive attitude towards life, and manifests itself in the ability to have peak experiences about little things. It is the feeling of inner peace, outer glow, and contact with a sense of meaning within our spirit. It might take the form of noticing the opening of blossoms in the spring, glorying in the fresh smell of an autumn evening, or reveling in the comfortable sensation of a big chair and a good book after a long day's work. Joy is connected with a heightened sense of awareness and the increased experience of all of our senses: smell, taste, touch, and so on. It exists with a sense of ultimate well-being, and fills the hours and days which have no "fun events." It's better than television because it is lived. It's the cherished "natural high" of the non-drug movement.

But spontaneous pleasure is very difficult to accomplish if you are locked into a low-key living-out of the rituals and routines of life. If you feel there is no pleasure in life, you must rediscover in yourself the Child who has been repressed. The Child is one of our basic ego-states—the one that is creative, experimental, spontaneous, emotional, and non-rational. The Child is the basis for your personal spontaneity, exuberance, and happiness.

But we've been so conditioned! We feel that in order to be mature, we must choke off all our spontaneity, worry about the appearance of our actions, be consistent, and be in control at all times. This can be taken to such an extreme it ruins happiness. Of course you have to be responsible for yourself, because you are an adult. But this doesn't mean you have to monitor or suppress every feeling and expression, and it never means that you cannot be emotional!

I try to break through all of this conditioning, and the habits of a dull and lifeless existence, by asking a person what he would do if he had fifty-thousand dollars a month—guaranteed. Perhaps he says he would really like to devote his time to photography. Then the question is this: could photography be a realistic alternative for you now? Are there ways you can make photography something that earns as well as something that is emotionally rewarding?

Most of the time, there is a way people can take their most fulfilling activities and turn them into careers. You may have to combine two or three things to make it work, but it is probably possible. But most people don't even try! Often they are so locked in to a job because it is "steady" or "certain," they are afraid to take the risk of changing

out of fear of economic hardship or uncertainty. They
seem to forget that emotional and internal rewards are
what really make life worthwhile. They forget they have
the freedom and the power to choose a new way of life.

What if you don't know what makes you happy? I recommend that you spend a year sampling many things, so
that you can find out. You needn't quit your job and go to
Europe to "find yourself." Why not gather together
catalogs from adult schools and craft centers and so on,
and pick out things to try? Try things, listen to yourself,
and *trust your gut level feelings*. This is really one of the
most reliable guides you have to yourself—your own
body. This is the only shrink you can listen to—your inner
feelings. Learn how to trust this inner feeling, and to respect it. Learn to say, "If my stomach, my gut, my body
language, says 'no,' then it's not for me." If something
excites you, and gives you a feeling of inner joy, then stick
with it—even if other people say it's foolish. If it gives you
joy, then you should do it. This is what forms the basis of
healthy motivation.

A lot of happiness is based on the enjoyment of doing.
Joy is derived from the process of doing, and is not contin-
gent on the end product. For example, the woman who
sews enjoys the dresses she makes, but she also enjoys the
actual sewing. If you are a photographer, you probably
enjoy taking and the developing of the pictures more than
you care about having the finished products hanging on
your walls.

Men sometimes have a slight disadvantage in learning
to enjoy life, because they frequently refuse to do things if
they feel they might not do them well. In our society, men
have traditionally been judged by the criterion of success;
and success has been measured by what they produce. It
may be then, that men are reluctant to produce anything
that (they fear) might reflect negatively upon themselves.
This is so confining! I urge men to just try new things,
without regard for "performance," to come into contact

with the exhiliarated feeling of doing things just for the excitement of *doing*. Women are usually somewhat freer to do this because society has generally judged them by their "femininity"—and our society has tended to consider a certain goofiness to be a feminine trait. This allows women to try all sorts of things, without the requirement that they be excellent at everything they do.

For a large number of people, enjoyment of life can be enhanced by simply breaking old habits of perception and behavior, and building new ones. You *can* change your attitude by focusing on the positive, listening to your inner feelings, and deciding you will give yourself permission to be exhuberent about life.

There are other people who are not so fortunate, and for them, the choice of joy is not enough. These people are locked into a glum, negative attitude towards life because they have a lot of deep inner hurt that has never been released. For such people, the hurt has to come out and be dealt with before they are fully free to choose to nourish their Child. Once the hurts are expressed, a sense of release often comes immediately. Then you can have an empty-chair dialogue with all the hurts you have identified; put each one in an empty chair, and examine them. No matter how much they hurt in the past, do you really need them now? Perhaps you can let go of some of them. If such hurts have kept your self-esteem low, then work on your sense of self-esteem. After the hurts are released and self-esteem is increased you can work to develop joy.

Putting Joy into Your Life

Joy is deep *internal* happiness. Joy is distinguished from fun, which is related to external events and activities. Fun takes place in groups and events; joy can be felt in solitude.

As is true in so many cases, people are often frustrated

by the definition of their own problems. For example, you may feel "joyless" partly because you have overblown notions of what "joy" is, and how much and how often you should experience it. No one feels joyful all the time. But you also shouldn't feel joyless all the time. It is a question of balance, and we are primarily concerned with developing and savoring the possibilities for joy which exist in each of our lives.

Ask yourself, "What makes me feel miserable? What prevents me from feeling joy?" Make a list of these obstacles, and then develop a plan of action to remove situations which block joy (make you feel miserable). In addition, ask yourself, "What gives me pleasure?" List these activities, and make a plan to include them in your daily life.

If you need to, set up a system for giving yourself permission to do the things which do make you happy. Chances are, you don't let yourself do these things often enough! A cookie jar is a good vehicle for doing this. Remember your childhood, when great pleasure came from being given a cookie from the cookie jar? Well, you are an adult now, and you don't need Mother to give you permission to have a cookie. So, set up your own cookie jar! Take slips of paper, and write down on each one an activity which you know gives you pleasure. For example, a long, soaking tub bath, a stroll through the woods, an hour at a health spa, or whatever you really enjoy doing. Put these in your cookie jar. Now, when you feel low, give yourself permission to raid the cookie jar. Pull out a slip of paper, and *do* what it says! You can also use this system to reward yourself for getting through tedious tasks— promise yourself a "cookie" when you finish. *Don't cheat yourself!* Carry out your promises to yourself, and give yourself rewards for doing so. Sometimes, you should raid the cookie jar just because you're feeling good and love yourself. Say to yourself, "I'm a pretty good person, and *I deserve* a cookie." In this way, you will begin to build into your life the very important *habit* of being good to yourself, and of seeing to it that you experience the little pleasures as well as the pains of daily existence.

Depression and Anger

We all say we are "depressed" at one time or another. In popular speech, "depression" refers to all varieties of low spirits, and perhaps to the general state of joylessness which I have already described. But if you take a closer look, you discover there is quite a difference between real depression and passing low spirits.

The depressed person complains of being tired all the time, even though he sleeps many hours. He is low on energy, interest, and enthusiasm. Often he wishes he could find something which would shake him up and get him out of his lethargy—but, he says, "nothing seems to be worth doing." As a result, nothing inspires in him a lasting sense of purpose, and he is continually bored. This is quite different from joylessness, which we have already discussed. In the case of joylessness, we need only learn to accept and nourish the Child within us; and when we do, the world becomes much rosier. The depressed person has more difficulty, because his Child is *angry,* and he is keeping the angry Child locked away from the world.

Whenever a person comes to me and complains of depression, I guide him to discover his anger, for anger and depression are intimately interconnected. If you deny or repress anger, depression results. It's basically that simple. When you finally express your anger, the depression begins to dissolve.

People who are afraid of their own feelings of anger usually develop this fear in childhood. There are many possible ways such a fear can be developed, but perhaps the most common relates to the parents' responses to the child's expression of anger. If parents automatically and uniformly punish a child for being angry, the child will eventually learn that anger is "unacceptable," and that if he wants love and support from his parents, he'd better repress his anger. If the child is thorough in his repression, he reaches the state where he is not even consciously aware of his anger. You might say that his system is screening it out, because anger is threatening to his safety and security. Children who aren't allowed—or helped— by their parents to express anger may also develop other fears. I have met adults who were afraid that if anger was allowed to come out, it would be uncontrollable. The emotion was perceived as having such destructive potential that it was repressed for fear it might cause the person to hurt or destroy others.

A very good example of this was a young woman who came to me in an extremely depressed state. After working with her for a while, it became apparent that her inner anger was directed towards her alcoholic mother. She had difficulty experiencing this anger, and could acknowledge it only on the intellectual level, saying, "Yes, rationally, I can see that I probably must be angry at Mother— somewhere underneath." She finally discovered the core of her repression: she was afraid if she ever openly expressed hostility towards her mother, her mother would die! This parent had effectively raised her daughter to believe that anger or hostility directed towards her was tantamount to matricide!

It is easier for people to get in touch with their inner anger if they can realize that anger is not necessarily a destructive emotion. It is destructive to repress it—the inability to express anger generally destroys one's capacity for intimate relationships which are happy and healthy, and can also contribute to depression. Obviously, there are destructive expressions of anger—suicide, murder, brutality, property damage, and so on. But there are also constructive ways of expressing anger, the the easiest of which is simply to say, "I am angry." Repeat this louder and louder, and accept the angry feelings you are experiencing. Then ask yourself, "How do I want to work out this anger?" You *do have* alternatives. If it is another person you are angry with, you can confront that person, and tell him of your feelings. You don't have to blame the other person for your anger (You *made me* angry. . . ."). Anger is an acceptable emotion, and you can take full responsibility for it. Simply say, "*I* am angry because. . ." How you express your anger is an individual thing. You can elect to work out your feelings by shouting in an empty room, pounding a pillow, taking vigorous exercise, writing in a journal, or expressing your anger in clay, color, or an art form. But remember, there was something that made you angry in the first place, and you have to deal with that. Look closely at what made you angry and deal with it.

Loneliness and Alienation

Avoiding solitude is a national pastime. Actually, time alone is very important time, and we all need it. Alone, we create ourselves, restore our spirits, and prepare ourselves for further intimacy.

There is a big difference between being alone and being lonely. You must become acquainted with this difference, for you may suffer from the misconception that you are "lonely" when actually you are simply alone. Develop your resources for turning alone-time into enriching and satisfying time. Also, do not feel there is "something wrong" if you want, need, and enjoy alone-time in the midst of your day. Many people think there is something wrong with their marriage just because they feel a repeated need for time alone—as if this would not happen in a "good" marriage! We all need alone-ness, although we each vary in how much we need. All of us must learn to use alone-time as an opportunity to enrich our lives and restore our spirits.

THE PLEASURES OF BEING ALONE

Using your journal, answer the following questions: How do you spend your alone-time? Do certain of your alone-time activities make you feel particularly blue? Particularly happy? Do you feel the need to punctuate your hours alone with contact with other people?

Make up a new plan for your alone periods. Omit, wherever possible, activities which make you feel especially blue—these, if necessary, can be done at another time, when you have company. Conversely, do include activities which give you pleasure. If, in your inventory, you discovered you tended not to undertake pleasureable activities in your alone-time, then look back over your journal writings about developing joy. Select some of the joy-producing activities on your list, and make the effort to include them in your time alone (i.e., "raid the cookie jar" often). View this as a delicious time for pleasuring yourself. Finally, if you feel a great need to break up your alone-time with contact with others, plan communication activities into your day: telephone one good friend, and write one long letter. If possible, make the larger commitment to use some of this time for volunteer work, or for taking a class—both of which will bring you into association with others.

Use a system of rewards—*liberally*—to help yourself break the old habits of alone-time blues. Give yourself a "cookie" everytime you look back over a period of aloneness and can see that you implemented parts of your plan. Congratulate yourself—you are changing for the better!

Herb, a successful engineer, could not bear to be alone. He had very low self-esteem, and needed constant contact with other people to reassure himself that he was really a "good person." Laughing and joking with others, he felt secure, because he could see their reaction to him. Alone, he had no external mirror to affirm his personal worth. After some time and work, Herb came to the point where he could finally say, "I'm a good person, and I like myself." Now he is no longer dependent on the outside world for proof of his personal value, and his compulsive socializing has subsided.

Another cause of loneliness is rooted in the feeling that no one cares, and you are not wanted. This usually develops in childhood, as a result of uncaring or unaffectionate parents. It is reinforced by the alienation characteristic of our metropolitan society today. People are alienated from each other. The sense of community has broken down, and many people have no sense of belonging. Families are broken up by divorce, or by vast distances, or whatever. Communities are transient, neighborhoods peopled with strangers. We have little sense of belonging to a larger group, a group that is concerned about us. Insofar as this is a fact of our social environment, we all must deal with greater or lesser feelings of alienation. You can seek to overcome the feeling that no one cares by working to build close meaningful relationships—within your family, with friends—and thus achieve a sense of belonging. However, in order to accomplish this, you must be willing to take risks: you must trust other people.

Distrust is a primary cause of personal loneliness. Many people are fearful of reaching out to others, and afraid of disclosing themselves. Again, this is the product of low self-esteem. People are afraid to let others see their weaknessess, fearing that this would invite ridicule or the withdrawal of affection. This refusal to open up is a strategy designed to insure safety—but it also guarantees isolation. If you need the constant admiration of others to convince you of your own worth, you can't disclose your human failings. Other people also admire those who can recog-

nize and accept their own weaknesses. By holding yourself back, you defeat forever the possible achievement of
your deepest needs: to be close to others, love and be
loved.

The fear of self-disclosure is connected with the sense of
having a *hidden self*. A person might feel that no one really
knows him, and that he is lonely. However, since he is
also convinced that anyone who discovers his "real self"
would reject him or laugh at him, it is not enough to simply avoid self-disclosure; he constructs a facade—a counterfeit self to parade as the real self. It is this "decoy" that
he falsely exchanges with others, passing it off as his inner
being. If he is successful at his counterfeit, he feels increasingly trapped by it—and increasingly alienated from other
people. Finally his self-hate turns on those he would have
admire or love him: ultimately the counterfeiter concludes,
"They are blind and foolish to think that this facade is
me."

Existential Loneliness

You must accept the fact that in an ultimate sense you
really *are* alone, no matter how many intimate relationships you have. You are born alone, and you die alone.
This is *existential loneliness*. There are experiences in life
you cannot share. For example, if you paint, you cannot
share your creative ecstasy with anyone else—you can
only report it, or describe it. You will always have a certain
aloneness, because you are the only person in the world
who fully knows and experiences YOU. Don't be afraid of
it. Allow yourself to get to know yourself.

Fear of Aging

We all know that our society worships youth, and this
knowledge is small comfort to the men and women who
anguish over the changes in their bodies and in their lives.

I sometimes think that if *Playboy* would shift its attention to mature love, and picture sensuous, beautiful, gray-haired men and women as the ideal, many people would unload their fixation on youth and breathe a sigh of relief. Much of our concern over aging is *artificial*, because it is based on a judgment of ourselves in relationship to a supposed ideal. Once we feel we have passed the ideal, nothing glorious remains, and the slow process of dying begins. Apart from the suffering produced, this orientation is tragic because it sets as the ideal a *static* life—fixed forever in one's twenties, forever tan, blonde and athletic (or whatever your ideal might be). But an unchanging life also means an absence of growing and experiencing all facets of a full life.

At the base of the fear of change is a fear of death. Every bodily change—sagging breasts, balding head, fading eyesight—is interpreted as a signal of one's mortality, a tangible reminder that life eventually ends. Of course life ends, there's no sense denying it. One cannot deny part of his own essence. Life is limited. If you can make peace with this, then aging loses its fearfulness and life will be *available* for living, rather than consumed by denying. It is a shame to waste so much time denying death when you could be using all that time and energy to enjoy living.

Life is limited, and also *dynamic*. This is the bargain—an offer which you cannot refuse, because there is no other. Growing up, falling in love, establishing a family—all of these are important and rewarding cycles in our lives. But so are later cycles. When children leave home, there is the opportunity for a new marriage relationship, free and private and relieved of the demands of parenting. Financial obligations can be shed, and therefore this is a time when one can return to school, or change to a career which is less rewarding monetarily but more fulfilling emotionally. This is a time with great possibilities for personal growth and enjoyment of life.

Similarly, retirement heralds another cycle of life, which

also offers its own riches. The saddest part of our culture, I think, is the misunderstanding of retirement. For so many people, this seems to mean stopping doing things. Of course, one stops working fulltime when he retires. But this should mean that he simply has more time to spend in the continuation of other interests. This is a shift, not an end. In retirement, one can be pleasure-oriented in a way that has not been possible since childhood. This is a mature age, a prime age.

Of course, many people can't make it through these later cycles of life because they tried to deny they would come and did not prepare for them. Therefore, when the children leave home, or when the retirement dinner is over, a great void looms. Life has become nothing, empty. The shock of the nothingness, after so many years of "running in harness," literally kills. Look at insurance company statistics, and you willl discover the awesome number of men who die within three years of their retirement.

The best prescription against this "shock of nothingness" is the development of an elastic concept of life. *You* are not equated with your children. *You* are not defined by your job. You are, instead, comprised of *many* filaments of interests, desires, responsibilities and capabilities. You must attend to this multi-dimensional you. No matter how important your work is, develop hobbies and pay attention to your family. No matter how much you love mothering or fathering, develop interests outside the home. In this way, if and when one of the filaments of your life breaks off, there are still others that continue to interest you and support your sense of worth and enthusiasm and

---

COME TO TERMS WITH AGING

In your journal, make a list of all the things that bother you about aging.

Going through your inventory item by item, make plans to do something about the aspects of aging which bother you. Of course, you must accept the fact that life and opportunities are limited—you cannot become 25 again if you are actually 70. But within realistic bounds, you can do much to make yourself feel good about you. If you have health problems, do what you can to get the best medical care available, and take the necessary steps to remain as healthy as possible—just as you would if you had a health problem at the age of 30. If you are bothered by graying hair, dye it. If you dislike your sagging body, then exercise, diet, and dress carefully to make your body feel and look as good as it possibly can. Keep in mind that you are doing these things not because you fear aging, but because you love yourself and want to feel good about yourself.

Carry out your plan! But as you carry out your plan, repeat again and again, "I like myself well enough that at each stage in my life I will adjust to whatever physical limitations come my way, knowing that this will enrich my life experience most." This simultaneous practice of action and attitude change is all-important. Attitude is really the key to lifelong happiness. You must like yourself, and like your age. If you can't achieve this, then none of the dyes or diets or dresses available can ever make you feel really good about yourself.

chapter 3

Focus on the Real You

In order to develop positive selfishness, you must be in contact with your inner feelings, desires, and fears. If you know your true inner self, you can make free, positive choices about the fulfillment of your own being. This self-knowledge must be based on unprejudiced self-exploration. Unfortunately, many people impose unnecessary constraints upon themselves by trying to conform to a perceived societal standard. Their false expectations and fears of self-acceptance become major barriers to the success of their quest.

"Measuring Up": The New Conformity

The most debilitating false expectation is that one must find a self which is "acceptable" to some *external* source of judgment. If the individual suffers from low self-esteem, this expectation is especially forceful. He feels he must find a self which "measures up" and thus proves that he is generally "worthy" as a person. By undertaking self-exploration fearing he will find a self that doesn't conform to some perceived standards, he is really limiting his search and his chance for meaningful growth.

The searcher is probably oriented to this concept of standards, which he feels he must measure up to. As he

begins his search for self, he automatically looks to see
what the relevant standards are, and he may find them by
taking his cues from the basic concerns of the growth
movement. Insofar as personal enrichment courses are
concerned with the topics of sensitivity, creativity, spontaneity, sensuality, relating, communicating, openness,
and so forth, the searcher may mistakenly conclude that
these concerns comprise a list of the qualities which *he*
should have in order to really find himself. He constructs,
thusly, a new standard for himself, and then suffers anxiety about measuring up to it. Thus, the search for self is
limited to the boundaries of what the searcher perceives as
"acceptable" by these external standards. It becomes a
struggle towards a new conformity.

   We must reject false expectations, and reaffirm that
one's central concern should be with his own individual
uniqueness, a recognition of his diverse personal choices,
and the actualizing of his dreams—without having to be
apologetic about whether or not those dreams "measure
up." The self-fulfilling person is one who has wishes or
dreams, is aware of his ambitions and talents, develops
the will to utilize his talents to their fullest in order to
realize his dreams, and doesn't feel badly about it. You can
begin your search for self-knowledge by becoming aware
of your desires. Do not worry about whether or not they
are "acceptable."

   Tom, a middle-aged man in one of my communications
classes, offers a good example of a person who worrys
about "acceptable" standards. Tom had graduated from a
military academy, and spent ten years as a career military
officer. Increasingly unhappy with his career, he finally
left the service and moved to California, where he enrolled
in a program of Business Administration. At the time I
knew him, he was finishing his degree and looking foreward to employment in the personnel department of a
major industrial concern. During one of our class sessions,

there was wide-ranging discussion of life goals, relating to society, and personal authenticity. Many of the students stressed the importance of abandoning the norms or standards of society in order to "do your own thing." In this context, they often criticized Tom as one who was unwilling to "free himself." Finally, Tom responded, "I *am* 'doing my own thing,' it's just that you don't like what my 'thing' is!" Tom was right. Fortunately, he was sufficiently self-confident to stand by his own desires and ambitions in the face of major questioning from others.

Contrast Kate to Tom. An intelligent and talented woman, Kate was an outstanding student in college, and had every opportunity to go on and earn her doctorate. Her family cannot understand why she dropped out of graduate school, and periodically questions why she "wastes" her talents being a housewife. Kate feels fulfilled as the mother of two youngsters. But she also feels guilty and inadequate. She is fulfilling her own desires, but has been made to feel that her goals and desires are "mediocre" or "unworthy." She apologizes for doing what she wants to do!

As these examples show, your first task in search of self is to discover what your desires and ambitions are, and *admit* them to yourself. After that, you can work on building the self-esteem and the will to use your talents to realize your personal life goals.

Goals—Materialistic and Otherwise

Much has been said about the value of rejecting materialism, and the development of new personal and social goals. This is extremely important, because many people have been conditioned to seek material possessions on the assumption that possessions *per se* will make them happy. Most of us, of course, know people who are miserable despite their beautiful homes, cars, boats, and clothes. One of the greatest tasks in the search of self is to discover what makes *you* truly happy. You may find that material things are not important at all, or are important only to a limited degree, in that they serve as a means to an end. This self-knowledge will help you keep sight of your priorities as you go through life.

It *is* true, however, that some people *do* seem to find happiness in material things, and are goal-oriented in a real sense when they seek success, or material possessions. There is a tendency to write off such people as being "unliberated" or "compulsive," when in fact they may be very self-fulfilling. If you find you really want a sense of luxury, and that this is what makes you feel fulfilled and lets you enjoy life, and if you honestly earn the money to buy beautiful things—then this is your dream. Fulfill it, your dream is not less worthy than that of the artist, who cares little about material possessions but desires fame and glory. We must not judge the goals people choose.

Our general value criteria flow in two directions, and it is good to be aware of these. On the one hand, there is the goal of personal fulfillment—the criterion here is *happiness*. On the other hand, there is the goal of improved societal existence—the criterion here is the *contribution* one makes towards bettering social interactions. The pursuit of individual happiness may coincide with making a contribution to social progress. But then again, it may not. We cannot expect or require each person to find his happiness through goals which contribute to the reform of society in an overt way. For the *individual*, the most important criterion in setting personal goals is, "Does this make me happy?" Coupled, of course, with the ethical considera-tion, "Does this *hurt* others?"

Relating

Many people have a need to overcome loneliness and alienation to be happy. We know that people need a sense of belonging and the ability to relate to others in meaning-

ful ways. This should not be misconstrued to mean that
there is something wrong with you if you also need a lot of
aloneness. Some people need greater amounts of time
alone than do others, in order to achieve personal happiness. They find their internal balance through separate
experiences, by removing themselves from interaction.
There is nothing abnormal or "inhibited" about their pref-
erence.

The growing feeling among some groups that the ex-
tended family, or "togetherness," is *better* must not be
made into a blanket value judgment. This would be an
injustice to the unique spirit of each individual.

We also place a great deal of importance on being
"open." Unfortunately, this word has been over-used,
and any specific meaning it might once have had has been
lost. Generally, the implication is that you are either
"open" or "uptight." Without hearing any definition of
these words, the listener (or reader) is very aware of the
connotations conveyed—open is better than uptight. But
what does it mean to be "open?"

You are open if you express your true thoughts and
feelings, and are receptive to the thoughts and feelings of
others. You are open if you disclose yourself to others. It is
important to cultivate flexibility of thought, and the ability
to disclose yourself—*when you want to*.

However, this is far too frequently misconstrued to
mean you have an *obligation* to be "open." Many people
feel that in order to measure up to the "standards" required of a "open person," they must disclose all their
thoughts and feelings to those with whom they interact.
This creates a special problem for one who values *privacy*,
for he is caught in a dilemma: if he respects his own desire
for privacy, he feels that he is a "closed" person—and
therefore has a serious shortcoming. On the other hand, if
he forces himself to disclose all, he suffers intense discom-

fort. All because of the misguided assumption that it is better to be open than to be anything else!

A Word on Becoming

We as individuals are dynamic. Life itself is fluid, and we are always in the process of changing and adapting. Thus, we are both being and becoming—being what we are, and becoming what we will be. This should be merely a comfortable truism. However, great emphasis on *becoming* can create nagging anxieties, by imparting to the individual the idea that he is never "enough."

If you seek your self, and focus too intensely upon the need to become more than you presently are (no matter what you currently are), you can create an inner despair which says, "I'll never measure up." This directly impedes the search for self by blocking your willingness to listen to your existing self. I once asked a certain young man why he didn't do the things he *wanted* to do, and he replied, "If I allow myself to follow my true personal desires, I would remain as I am, and that would mean that I'd never become all that I'm capable of becoming." This remark was made with great anxiety, illustrating this special concern about "becoming." Ironically, this is an anxiety that present happiness is dangerous to future happiness!

This kind of anxiety over "settling for less than I could be" drives people to go against their natural inclinations. Sometimes this is ultimately beneficial. For example, you might be fearful to run for public office, because you're not sure you can speak before large audiences. However, if you push yourself to try, you may discover that you can do it, and your self-confidence jumps up ten degrees. Or, perhaps you're afraid to talk about personal problems, so you keep all your worries inside yourself and suffer terrible headaches. You just might find that if you push your-

self to overcome your fears, you can learn to communicate
your anger and desire to others, and the stress in your life
is reduced.

However, you have to respect yourself to know when
"pushing yourself to overcome" is productive, and when
it is counterproductive. If you enjoy privacy and need a lot
of time alone, but feel that you *should be* more open in
relating to others more, you're headed for unhappiness.
Pushing yourself to overcome preferences which enhance
your happiness is counterproductive, and if you do it, it's
only because you have been subtly brainwashed into
thinking that it is "best" to become something other than
yourself.

Creativity

Here again we see the power of a word that has been
overworked by popular sloganeering in recent years. We
have emphasized the importance of doing meaningful
things in a creative way. But who's to say what is creative?
And if you aren't a painter, potter, or poet, are you locked
into an "uncreative" existence?

I once told a young woman that she didn't have to be an
artist in order to be creative. Reassuringly, I explained to
her that Abe Maslow had acknowledged that people could
be creative, even if they just stayed home and cooked, and
that a first-rate soup is more creative than a second-rate
painting. She was quick to retort that this didn't help her
at all, and in fact increased the anxiety she felt, because it
demanded she become *first-rate* at something! Why, indeed,
should you have to worry about making a first-rate anything in order to call yourself creative and therefore find
self-esteem? Enjoy *doing* whatever you like to do, and find
self-esteem in the fact that you are capable of enjoyment,
and of realizing your own desires. This requires self-
knowledge, will, and sometimes strength—surely these
are sufficient bases for self-respect.

One Man's Meaning

Whatever you do, don't let others define for you what is "meaningful." This is the surest way to transfer effective judgment of your worth from you to other people. Many people make the mistake of assuming that "meaning" is monolithic, or absolute, and that it has the same content for all humans. This simply is not true. There may be some absolute *ethical values* which pertain to all humans—for example, the ethical obligation that a parent has to see to the welfare of an infant which he has brought into this world.

However, ethics are not our question here. The important point is that ethics and "meaningfulness" are not always synonomous. You may conclude that you have a certain set of ethical values—for example, the obligation to care for yourself and your children, to do the best you can in this world, to avoid harming others, to share your good fortune with those less fortunate, and so on. These values set the parameters for your behavior, they set outer limits, so to speak. These values are meaningful to you, in that it is important to you to live by your ethical code.

On the other hand, your quest for meaning in life might be much more specific in focus. *You* might find meaning in working to improve the environment for the next generation, through volunteer work and political activity. Someone else, who shares your general ethics, might find meaning in family life—working to build a good home, be a good parent, create a strong and loving bond within a large family. His meaningfulness is not less than yours, nor is yours less than his. Meaning is intrinsic to the actor, and is fulfilled as it is acted upon. This concept of meaning is central to the definition of the self-fulfilling person: one who acts to realize his desires, without apology, and thereby fulfills his sense of meaning, utilizes his talents, develops his will to act, and enhances his sense of personal strength.

Strength

People in search of self are often concerned about personal strength, wanting very badly to be "strong," and fearing that they are not. Actually, the fact that they set forth to "find themselves" shows their capacity for strength and the will to improve life. If strength is lacking, it is usually the strength to be the judge of one's own actions, and a dependence on the opinions of others. Fortunately, this power can be recovered, and this strength built through building self-esteem.

There is a common tragedy relating to the issue of strength. Many people are so concerned about "being strong," and not being "dependent" (which they see as a weakness) they cut off all meaningful relationships! Marlene is a good example of this pattern of behavior. Divorced at thirty, Marlene went through considerable turmoil establishing herself as a single, professional woman. When she succeeded, she was determined to keep her strength and independence at all costs. She met and dated John, fell in love, and was happy—until she "realized" that this was a sign of her "weakness." She then became determined to break off with John, because she was frightened by the idea that her happiness was dependent on being with another person! As a result, she retained her "independence" (the symbol of her "strength") and was very unhappy.

Marlene's behavior illustrates the confusion of dependence and interdependence. All relationships which are loving and caring take away from us the state of being "free as a bird." If you love someone, and commit yourself to a life with him, or her, then you are not fully independent. But you *are free*. You are free, because you *chose* to make the commitment. You, as a free individual, decided to endorse the relationship. This was your independent act. The relationship you have chosen is interdependent. In order to keep it fulfilling both you and your partner, you must be willing to nurture it; you must tend not only to your own feelings, but also those of your spouse. You have an obligation to do this in order to keep yourself happy. Conversely, if you no longer wish to have this obligation, perhaps it is time for the relationship to end.

Severing a relationship because you feel you are dependent on the happiness it gives you is a mistake. Such an act is false; if anything, it signifies a lack of strength, for true strength allows you to do the things that make you happy, and to avoid the pitfalls of fear. Certainly, you can continue to break off every caring relationship which gives you joy, but you will go on and find another relationship, and another, and another. So why not take this knowledge and say to yourself, "Well, I'm not *dependent* on this relationship, because I know I would live without it and eventually I would find someone else. But I am happy with my mate, and he with me. We are interdependent for happiness. I am a free individual, and I choose to stay. I will use my strength to build and nurture my love, and I will know it is not weakness to derive joy from a deep commitment to another person."

Personal Authenticity

"Be authentic!" Be yourself, and don't be a counterfeit. Don't feel you have to hide behind a mask and be what someone else wants you to be.

To some people personal authenticity means they should stand by their convictions and never compromise. Other people place great value on compromise and accommodation, and emphatically are *not* "betraying themselves" or "being phoney" in their willingness to compromise on their beliefs and preferences. We must respect both approaches, and refrain from making blanket judgments regarding which is "superior." The superior behavior is that which is right for the individual involved.

Even when one seeks to be fully authentic, you can

carry it too far. The best guide is often found in the golden rule. I have often seen authenticity used as a justification for cruelty, and as a rationalization for a total lack of civility. If being rude and disregarding common manners is what you feel like doing, then I suppose that is your business. But you have an obligation *to yourself* to be aware. Be in touch with your feelings and motivations, and if you discover that you feel antagonistic towards another person, it might be worthwhile for you to explore that feeling, and understand it. If you simply "act out" your hostilities, giving yourself permission by saying, "I'm merely being real and authentic," you will let off the steam, but you will never confront the fire. You may be better off than the person who represses anger totally, but you are not in touch with the cause of your anger or hostility, and therefore remain divorced from your inner self.

The call to "be real" has fueled a popular disregard for conventional etiquette. I make no judgment here, except to assert the right of a person to continue to cherish and observe traditional polite manners if he chooses to do so. This does not necessarily mean that he is "uptight" and in need of more spontaneity; it may mean that he is very much aware of his own desires and preferences, and acts to realize them. One of my acquaintances faces this problem all the time. Her desire is to have a gracious home, and to set a beautiful table when she entertains. She does this not because she feels she will be criticized if she doesn't, and not because she needs to impress people, but because *she* enjoys the feeling, sight, and smell of a lovely room decorated with flowers, candles, and good food. This gives her a positive experience. Nevertheless, she constantly encounters the implication from others that she is doing this because she "feels she has to," and that she should "relax." It seems that the contemporary assumption is that a person who behaves in traditional ways is "uptight." How much unhappiness this causes! If my acquaintance were to give in to the implications of others, and serve hasty dinners on paper plates, she would lose a major source of enjoyment in her life.

Sex Roles: Masculine/Feminine

Men and women today can find and fulfill themselves in a variety of roles. The women's movement has opened up a wide range of choices for women who wish to seek fulfillment in careers outside the home. This movement has also sparked the beginning of a more general human liberation movement, and the concept of "men's lib." Men are beginning to realize they do not have to be burdened with the task of being sole breadwinner for their families, and that they do not have to be constrained by the traditional (social) concepts of "masculine" behavior. This has allowed men to experience and display emotions relating to insecurity, fear, and caring to a greater extent than was before "acceptable."

The family roles of husband and wife have also been greatly affected. Many women have refused traditional marriage, and have sought to write new contracts, freeing themselves from the sole obligation of caring for the house, making beds, and watching the children. When the redefinition of roles reflects honest and free choices made by both partners, this is positive, healthy, and assists each to achieve self-fulfillment.

There are, however, side-effects of the general redefinition of male and female roles in our society. To the extent that this social change is highly publicized and acclaimed by well-known people, it produces great pressure on individuals to go along with it. I do not mean to say that psychologists or feminists are preaching conformity to a new set of role concepts. I am saying that our society creates pressures towards conformity—if a young person perceives new role concepts to be "in," he will feel pressure to adopt them.

Much has been written about the difficulties of the individual who chooses the non-conformist's role. Today, these difficulties also arise when the individual really desires to fit into the traditional role. He feels guilty of this! This is particularly evident in young women who have strong desires to fulfill themselves by staying at home with their children. Jeanne explained the guilt she felt in the following way: "I really like my life right now. I have a lot of interests—sewing and quilting and playing tennis. I read a lot, and spend time with my three-year old. When Todd comes home from work, I have the dinner ready, so we can eat right away and have the evening to ourselves. I really don't like the idea of leaving my child with a babysitter all day, and rushing home at five-thirty to start dinner. Even if Todd helped me, it would mean that we'd eat late, and then, of course, we'd both be anxious about giving the baby enough of our time." So what is wrong with Jeanne? She feels guilty. As she puts it, "I feel like a slug, you know, one of those slimy little creatures that live off someone else, and don't do anything productive. I get this feeling whenever someone says to me, 'How do you like staying home, doing nothing?' Or someone else will say, 'Don't you feel like a parasite living off your husband?' Society seems to regard me as having no ambition and no worth because I'm not out bringing home a paycheck we don't need." Jeanne is very bitter about the attitudes of women in particular. "Why can't some of us choose to stay home, without being made to feel we're lesser beings? If some women don't like the traditional women's role, then I'm all in support of their right to get out and pursue a profession. But why do those career women sneer at 'little housewives?' You'd think that they were the only people in the world who are worthwhile!"

Jeanne has a point. The woman who prefers to stay home is not of "lesser value" than the woman who works, just as the woman who has a menial job is not of lesser value than the professional woman. The real goal is the freedom to choose what is right for ourselves.

Men also have the right to choose. The man who wants a woman to perform the traditional wifely role while he exercises traditional male prerogatives should not automatically be branded a "chauvinist pig." If this is what *both* he and his wife choose as their style of marriage, then it is the most fulfilling marriage *for them*. Outsiders who criticize such a marriage are really the agents of conformity. Perhaps "being conventional" is becoming the unconventional mode of life!

Freedom to Be

What I have tried to do is make the reader aware of the dangers of assuming that any one set of values are the proper values for all individuals. To actualize our unique potential, each person must be free to be himself. This means that he must be free to choose his own roles and values, without constraint by a society that fosters conformity. If the individual chooses to be alone, we must not brand him as "alienated." If he prefers privacy to togetherness, he is not to be regarded as "closed." The freedom to choose means having the freedom to select a mode of life. Through an honest choice, the individual actualizes his desires, finds meaning, and retains true authenticity.

chapter 4

Developing Positive Selfishness

The development of positive selfishness involves self-awareness, self-acceptance, self-esteem and self-assertion. In fact, many approaches to personal growth address these very topics, in this specific sequence. Logically, this makes great sense, for self-awareness and self-acceptance are prerequisites for self-esteem; and self-esteem is essential to self-assertion. However, logic does not always indicate the easiest approach, especially when we are dealing with complex human emotions. I have actually found that the logical path is often the most difficult—especially if you suffer from low self-esteem at the outset.

Self-awareness through self-disclosure is not the optimum beginning. Low self-esteem involves a poor self-image, which must be at least partially disarmed before the individual can open himself to productive self-disclosure. Otherwise, the only things he will disclose about himself are the elements of his negative self-view. This is such a painful and seemingly futile beginning that it discourages one from wanting to know more of himself—in fact, it can reinforce his notion that this is all there is to know, and make his self-image worse than before.

It is also generally difficult to attempt full self-acceptance as the intitial step towards growth and change. This again devolves to the unfortunate fact that many who suffer low self-esteem are truly accomplished in the art of hating themselves. Since they do see themselves as despicable, it is frightening and discouraging for them to be told to accept themselves as they are. This is received as a message that they will always be the contemptible person they think they are, and discourages any desire to introspect further.

As you see, the path to personal growth is not an easy, grand sweep through nice logical stages leading to self-respect. It must be found gradually through a series of "split stages," with personal fears disarmed and self-confidence built at the very outset. A small diagram might clarify my own approach.

Step	Task
Self-Esteem 1	build some love for yourself.
Self-Acceptance 1	determine that you won't be injured by having some negative traits.
Self-Awareness	find out what your body tells you how you feel, and what you want.
Self-Acceptance 2	don't fight what *is*, but accept it; make some determinations to change those things you don't like; love yourself despite your shortcomings.
Self-Esteem 2	respect yourself **as a total** person; take responsibility not just for your actions and "obligations," but for making yourself happy. Commit yourself to yourself.
	(Note: The definition of happiness must be personal—for some it may be love, for others, travels or money.)

Self-Esteem 1: *Building Self-Love*

If you hope for self-respect and inner peace, you must love yourself. Even if you don't now love yourself, this is the easiest first step for you to take—gradually—because we all *want* to love ourselves. Loving yourself is not negatively selfish or conceited; it is responsible, mature, and the key to personal growth.

LIKING PARTS OF YOURSELF

Although you may not like all of you, and you may feel ambivalent about yourself, you must build up an awareness of those aspects of yourself that you do like, and learn to retreat to these when your doubts become too great. Many people start with such low self-esteem! If need be, list just one thing you like about yourself. Then, even if you have named the smallest thing, tell yourself, "I must be pretty good, if I have this." This affirmation of the positive has an important effect, because if you have felt ashamed of some of your "negative" qualities and afraid of acknowledging them, you can now see that "negative" things are not the only defining aspects of your self. You, like all mortals, have a mixture of positive and negative qualities.

Next, start adding to your list, emphasizing the positive. Don't try to weigh the positive things you find to see if they are "out numbered" by the negative. Your task is simply to find things about yourself that you do like. Say to yourself, "If I have these things, then don't I deserve more pleasure?" Play the loving and indulging adult who is rewarding a child for something good, and *give yourself a pleasure*. Perhaps as a pleasure you may give yourself permission to treat yourself to a new coat, a trip to the seashore, or a lazy day. It doesn't matter, as long as it is pleasureable to you. Enjoy it, don't cheat yourself out of it, because pleasure reinforces more pleasure. When something feels good, it makes you want (and feel you deserve) more of it. Find this self which takes pleasure in life, and affirm yourself for contacting it. Make the effort to cater to it.

Once you have in mind a firm list—however short—of the qualities in yourself that are good, you are ready to attempt an initial acceptance of your "negative" (but human) aspects as well.

Self-Acceptance 1

We learn early in our lives that certain traits in our personality are acceptable and others are not, that some traits will bring us praise and approval, while others bring punishment or disapproval. We have, all of us, to accept the fact that we cannot be "all good."

If you see yourself as being kind, loving, giving and happy, these are easy qualities to accept because they bring you positive feedback. But self-awareness and self-acceptance involve knowing and embracing the totality of you, including the "bad" qualities you sometimes display, such as hostility, anger, fear, anxiety and loneliness. The first step towards self-acceptance is to admit that you have a "negative list" of qualities, and to see that this is natural and does not threaten your basic worth as a person. Being afraid or ashamed because you have negative emotions is self-destructive and totally non-productive.

After you have learned to affirm your positive traits, you can begin to work on the idea that the negative side of you is not dangerous to your self-esteem. This can begin as an intellectual exercise. First, you can reaffirm the fact that nobody is perfect, and you are being not only harsh but also unreasonable if you demand perfection of yourself. Second, you can begin to think about the possibilities of using negative traits as constructive elements in your search for self—as guideposts in helping you discover what experiences or problems produce them or bring them out.

As an example, let's say you feel lonely, and you are ashamed of this because you view your loneliness as a sign of your personal weakness. Tell yourself, "OK, this is my time to focus on myself. I need this loneliness in order to help me become more aware of myself. This motive, this *use* of my loneliness, is positive and constructive." Or, as another example, assume that you have an inner anger. Don't run away from it and try to pretend it's not there.

Instead, use it as a path to inner awareness. If need be, accentuate the anger in an effort to find the connection to what you are angry about. Ask yourself why you are angry. What happened to make you angry? What constructive way can you think of to deal with it? We're so very afraid to be angry! Yet anger is good because it helps us come into contact with our conflicts and dissatisfactions, and these cannot be dealt with until they are discovered and defined.

A NEW VIEW OF YOUR "NEGATIVE" QUALITIES

One easy exercise you might try with yourself is to make a quick (and short) list of your negative traits. Then consider the possibility of *renaming* each item on the list!

In my experience, it seems that many people are the prisoners of words—words which they apply to themselves, and then suffer because those words hurt them. Do you consider yourself "over emotional?" Why not call it "sensitive?" Do you consider yourself "uptight?" Call it "concerned." If you've been thinking that you are "paranoid," rephrase your thinking and tell yourself you're anxious. As you can see, the word you choose to apply to yourself has a life of its own. Don't you feel better to say that you are "anxious, sensitive and concerned" than to say that you're "over-emotional, uptight and paranoid?" To rephrase your self-descriptions is not a mere exercise in rationalization. Generally, persons who apply terrible adjectives to themselves suffer from too dark a view of self—not from a tendency to overlook weaknesses. You won't be kidding yourself, you will be giving yourself a break—a fresh chance to get past the barriers of labels and look at yourself.

In the beginning, a certain element of courage is required to look unflinchingly at the positive-negative totality of which you are comprised. Focusing on the negative within you can lead to positive results, if done with a complete absence of judgment. You can be brave enough to look at yourself as fully as currently possible, admitting that all of it is you.

POSITIVE-NEGATIVE SELF-DISCLOSURE

The following is an exercise that will help you to start getting in touch with, and accepting, both the positive and the negative aspects of your personality. While using these guidelines in your quest for self, you must be honest with yourself, accepting the complete truth in all that you experience about yourself. Do *not* judge, however; simply examine. Avoid any grading or evaluating of your personality. Statements like, "I know it's bad, but often I'm angry and bitter," should be changed to, "Often I'm angry and bitter." Avoid resolutions to change for the moment.

To help you with this exercise, a tape recorder is essential. If you do not own one, borrow or rent one; above all, do not deny yourself this valuable experience by deciding that obtaining and preparing the machine "isn't worth it." It is!

Put yourself in this situation: You have just met someone you have always wanted as a close friend—let us call him Mr. X. Quickly run through those qualities you like about yourself that you would relate to such a person. Try to offer him only positive, constructive facts and opinions as they flow freely. Use your own name. You might begin by saying something like this:

"Ruth is 5' 7" tall, and she weighs 140 pounds. She doesn't like to be that heavy, so if she were asked, she might cheat a little and say she weighs 135. I don't know why, but for some reason that would help her self-confidence. However, I have to give her credit. She's really trying to lose those five extra pounds. It's just an insignificant little problem she has right now. She's been told often enough she has a nice figure. Anyway, Ruth has a lot of good qualities. For instance, she_____. On the other hand, she is insecure in some areas, and maybe even dishonest with herself at times. For example, she'll fake it if somebody asks her_____. Maybe she doesn't want to admit her feelings of insecurity, so she overcompensates by coming on too strong, pretending to be a bit *too* competent, and sometimes she even says and does things that later on seem to be_____."

Allow this monologue all the time necessary. In essence, what you are attempting to do is present an honest portrait about who and what you are.

Next, while leaving the recorder on, assume that Mr. X has just said to you, "But now, I want to hear about the negative side of you." Answer his request, describing as many of your negative qualities and feelings as you can. It might go something like this:

"Well, Ruth is basically a coward. I guess I'm really afraid to confront people I admire, so I cater to them, and I try to buy their love. I know I'm prostituting my integrity when I do that, but isn't everyone like that? I actually lie sometimes to please others, but what's wrong with wanting to be accepted and admired? No, I don't like this part of me. Not only that—and I've never admitted this to anyone before—but sometimes I feel as if_____."

When you have finished this negative disclosure, with the machine still on, present a dialog to Mr. X between the positive and negative sides of your inner self. It might sound like this:

"Well look, I'm no different from everybody else. Sure, I have hang-ups and fears and problems, but show me somebody who doesn't! I haven't even mentioned that I feel that life is_____ and I don't like_____ and I catch myself being worried and even depressed when I realize that I_____. Because of talking like this, I realize some of the parts of me I'd like to change. Why? Certainly it's not because I *should*. I just figure I'd be a happier person if I did. I'd be more comfortable with myself if I did—that's why. I'd be a better friend to myself, not to mention others. I guess I've always wanted to change those things. But not for you—for me!"

With pencil and paper, seated near a clock with a sweep second hand, it is now time to replay the tape. Avoid an embarrassed reaction; it is only you, being honest. Go back and time the number of words per minute as you describe your positive self. Then go forward on the tape and do the same sort of timing as you describe your negative self. Pay careful attention to the differences and changes of speed, pitch, and volume in your voice while you praise yourself and describe the things you admire, as opposed to the sections where you discuss your faults. Is there a significant difference? Is it revealing?

Most people will slow down when they talk about their negative "secrets." Those repressed and painful experiences in your life have been locked behind an iron door, imprisoned a long time. Pain retreats and fades as soon as you begin to confront it. Encourage yourself to relive those feelings as you hear them again. Admit they exist. Exchange places with them, becoming their master instead of their slave. As you work your way through self-awareness towards self-esteem you will cease to be the slave.

Self-Awareness

Now that you have worked through the preliminary steps to self-esteem and self-acceptance, you can begin to work on self-awareness, since now you have lowered the barriers which otherwise blocked your ability to explore the inner self.

What is self-awareness? It is being alive and awake to your own needs, desires, feelings and wishes; it is knowing yourself in an unlimited sense. How do we build awareness of who we are? Through three levels: our body, our feelings, and our mind.

Body-Awareness

Most of our communication is non-verbal, and we all use body language naturally and automatically. It is relatively easy to become aware of the body signals others are sending us. For example, if someone encourages you to talk, but at the same time taps his fingers and continually looks at his watch, you very readily get the real message—he is eager to end the communication, or at the very least, he is not fully "there." We all pick up body-language messages given by others, and readily interpret scowls, smiles, tears, and blushes. However, we can also look to our *own* bodies to give us messages. This is a very valuable form of communication with self. Your body is always there sending you messages, but you must learn to receive them. You must be open to the messages it gives you, and learn to interpret them.

The body is the mirror of the self, and tells us about our changes of mood. When we are happy, our eyes brighten; when we are anxious, our muscles tighten, and so on. As you begin to become aware of your body's responses, it is important to remember that whenever there is an incongruency between verbal language (what you say) and body language (how your body reacts), it is the body that tells the truth! The body's responses are involuntary, and therefore, it cannot lie. Words can be false, we can pretend and deceive even ourselves, but our bodies speak the true state of our inner being. Thus, it is very important for the person who is seeking self-awareness to spend a great deal of time paying attention to his bodily responses—to find the incongruities between body and words, and to seek and understand the reasons these incongruities exist.

In order to become acquainted with your body's messages, I recommend you set aside an unpressured time every day, perhaps fifteen minutes, when you can relax and concentrate on your body.

Find any part of your body which feels pained or tense, and then focus on that. For example, let's say you become aware that your lower abdomen is tight. Focus on your lower abdomen and try to relax it. As it begins to tighten up again, relax it again. Be aware of your thoughts and emotions as you do this, and see if there is a particular problem or worry playing on your mind. This problem is probably related to the tightness in your abdomen. Use the time to work on that problem; have a dialogue with the different aspects of it ("I should do this" vs. "I don't want to do that" or "I'm afraid this will get worse" vs. "I'm silly to worry about it"). The I-message (*I feel* such-and-such) must have a dialogue with the you-message (You *should* do_____. You *can't* do_____.). As you continue the dialogue, you may not completely resolve the problem— but you will begin to resolve your feelings about it and you will find your body's tension relaxing. By using this technique, you can acquaint yourself with the meaning of your body's messages. Soon you will be able to listen to your body in a dynamic way—that is, it will help you to know how you "really feel" about things as they happen, instead of your having to work so hard to decipher your feelings!

I have encountered people who object to this method of coming into contact with feelings, saying, "Fine, I have a backache. But how do I know what problem this links to?"

Here is the point where the mind—the intellect—comes into play. You can intellectually review all the possibilities of what might be bothering you. Go through the entire list and work on resolving each one. After each one, rub your back and say, "Well, that's over. I'm glad that's taken care of." Now, it's true you won't always be able to resolve all your problems this way, but you can work this way on clarifying your feelings. This is the first step towards realistic problem-resolution.

It's unfortunate, but many people have the idea that if something is bothering you (for example, a little backache), you should try to ignore it, or do something to "take your mind off it"—something to make yourself feel better. This is a mistake. You should look into the problem, even if you feel that you're wallowing in it and feeling increased pain. You must get in touch with the problem, because this is the key to getting rid of it. Many people think that wallowing in a problem is "immature." This is a product of our socialization. We are told, "You must be strong, you must overcome your weaknesses, you must not dwell on your problems." This is the barrier that has to be overcome before you can really become self-aware. You can only be aware of yourself through your body, and so you must pay attention to it, and regard this as a form of "meeting the problem head-on."

Of course, when you focus on your body, you must try to relax. Do some relaxation exercises, inhale and exhale slowly, and bring yourself to a state of calm. Then begin to become aware of body feelings and keep asking yourself, "How do I feel now?" Soon you will begin to make connections between body and feelings.

There is a pitfall here, too. Many people think they feel good all the time, and become depressed when they realize they really feel tired, aching, or tense. *Accept* the fact that you don't feel good. Then comfort your body. Ask yourself, "What are the things that bother me?" There

is nothing wrong, or "immature" about feeling bad—
except that it hurts and is not pleasureable.

The Self in Conflict

As you become increasingly aware of your inner existence,
you will discover (probably with some consternation) that
there is more than one "inner you," and that these inner
selves are often in conflict. This is quite natural.

Fritz Perls, founder of the Gestalt therapy method, describes the conflicting powers within us as the "Top Dog"
and the "Under Dog." Top Dog is the rational, manipulating, organizing self who is continuously in conscious
command. Top Dog tells you what you *should* do, *should*
think, how you *should* behave. Under Dog, however, responds to your *feelings*, your needs and desires. Ultimate
success is in the achievement of the whole of you becoming integrated. It is then that you have reached an inner
equilibrium.

In the process of knowing our inner selves, each of us at
times experiences an unpleasant impasse of feelings, a
constellation of emotions that are conflicting, pulling us in
opposite directions. "I'm torn between doing it and not
doing it!" is a familiar phrase and feeling to us all. Such a
state leaves you without the power to make an adequate
decision about how to respond or what to do. We become
immobilized when a conflict seems to have no answer.

Part of the power gained in attaining self-knowledge is
your ever-increasing awareness of the divergent forces
unceasingly at work within you. Often the conflict is between the rational and controlling Top Dog in opposition
to the submissive and insecure Under Dog.

Through Gestalt role playing, you are consciously acting
out both selves, carrying on a dialog between them. It is
important to see yourself as an equally assertive individual
within each state of being—both while you are Top Dog as

well as when you are Under Dog. Should you allow in-
equality to exist, it would be as if you had bribed a boxer;
you would then know ahead of time exactly who would
win.

Often there are more than two aspects of your inner self
in conflict. In this event, you experience something like a
free-for-all—two teams, or whole armies attacking one
another. Visualize such a contest with no referee, no um-
pire, and no rules, and it is easy to see why chaos reigns.

This situation is changed immediately, however, to the
degree that you become aware of this inner arena. Consciously experiencing that struggle will afford you
insight—a useful form of insight that will result in sufficient self-confidence for you to seek out a resolution.
Trusting what you experience at a "gut level," accepting
intuition and whatever "feels right," is an advantageous
approach. These Under Dog forces have tremendous
power and a considerable ability to lead you toward the
realization of what you *could* be and *want* to be, as opposed
to what you perceive you *should* be. The standards of others, your parents' code, or Top Dog's demands are not
always correct for you.

OPEN DISCUSSION WITH YOUR INNER CONFLICTS

Allow the conflict between Top Dog and Under Dog to
take place in an open discussion. Assign a seat to each.
Then, take the seat you have assigned to Top Dog. Let him
talk aloud through you and express his views freely, just
as he has done silently within you all your life. Accept his
reasonable arguments. "You should work harder toward
the goals of making money and achieving security," he
might say. "You should be a better person, strive for perfection, do what others expect," he will continue. "You
should listen to me exclusively, and you won't make mis-

takes. You shouldn't worry. You should simply do what's right."

Now, change chairs for an obverted view, and verbalize what Under Dog feels. Perhaps you will notice that the simple act of moving from one chair to the other is suddenly difficult. The reason is simple. Under Dog is submissive by nature and accustomed to being fought down and beaten, and he is now being asked to speak! He feels just as you once did when you had to address an audience for the first time. Hesitantly, of course, Under Dog might well begin by noting, "That Top Dog's favorite word seems to be *should*, but there are really so many other points of view. To be honest, I must admit that my favorite word is *feel*. I can't deny it; I feel comfortable *feeling* things. I know it's not a very popular approach around here, but I *feel* I'd just like to relax, take life as it comes, and enjoy my daily experiences. I'd like to express myself more creatively somehow. I suppose basically I'm an artist . . . but I often wonder why I'm always told that's so bad. I don't need money and power and authority to make me happy. I'm happy now, just with what I already have. I feel secure now. My goal in life is simple; I merely feel as if I want to participate."

Because Top Dog is strong and aggressive, he can logically be expected to disapprove and interrupt. Allow this, but also allow Under Dog to defend his position adequately. "Yes," Under Dog could respond, "I see the logic and truth in what you're saying. You give very good advice, and I don't deny you your place. But now that you bring it up, why do you always deny *me* and *my* place . . . ?" Let the two of them discuss this matter at length. Perhaps the conversation between them will become so lively that you will no longer have the time or need to change chairs. When that happens, relax in your front-row seat, and watch the performance. Allow *them* to arrive at a breakthrough and a compromise.

Send them off-stage and objectively consider their solutions. If you decide both emotionally and rationally that the conflict between the two of them for the moment has been thoroughly discussed and resolved, act upon it. Unless it feels unconditionally right, however, the dialogue was ended too soon.

Repeat this exercise whenever the sense of being unconditionally right escapes you. In the beginning this feeling may occur often, but like any habit, returning to the confrontation becomes easy and automatic in time. Intercommunication between Top Dog and Under Dog will soon develop its own set of signals and language. Bring the two of them on to talk of new things freely and often—being certain, of course, which one is professing what view. Let them arrive at a new compromise. This is part of the totality of successfully achieving a complete personal experience.

DISCOVERING YOUR CURRENT EGO NEEDS

An important part of self-awareness consists of discovering your current ego needs. To help you do this, think of some people who, in your estimation, have most completely arrived at a comfortable level of self-acceptance and self-fulfillment. Make a list of their qualities, even if that person evolves into an "ideal you" rather than one or more of the people you know. Make your list as complete as possible, writing down each element of *successful living* as it enters your mind.

Once the list is complete, study it closely and decide which single item of top priority you would choose to head a revised list. Continue this new list, putting the second most important item next, then the third. In the process of creating this new order of values, you may find that you have omitted an important item in the preliminary list. Add it in its proper position and continue. You may also find that an original item might well be dropped or combined with one of the others. Work with this second list until you feel confident that you have compiled all your major needs and desires in their proper order.

Your first list, in spontaneous random order as the items first come to mind, might read like this:

1. Success at work
2. Unlimited wealth
3. Feeling superior
4. Ability to relax
5. Contentment at the end of day
6. Being popular; having more friends
7. No problems
8. No worries
9. Love from my family
10. Respect and admiration
11. Fame, applause, parties
12. Being more attractive
13. Being smarter
14. Changing my life style; escaping

Before reading further, write your own spontaneous list of needs and desires. Close the book at the end of this paragraph, and write them down as quickly as possible. Once your own preliminary list is complete, study it and revise it, choosing the order of importance in which these items should appear. Discard, combine, or include any new ones, and then compare it with your original list. How does it differ? *Close the book and begin.*

Returning once more to the above suggested list, reconsider the items given by a hypothetical person. Revised into a second statement of priorities, the list might resemble this:

1. Self-fulfillment
2. A feeling of health and happiness

3. Inner peace
4. Ability to solve problems
5. Enjoyment of all life's opportunities
6. Acceptance by family
7. Acceptance by friends and co-workers
8. Improving my physical and mental potentials
9. Absence of guilt or shame

Notice the differences between the above two lists, and compare as well the two you have written. The first is usually longer. It also indicates what your strongest current desires probably are, rather than reflecting long-term needs. Such a list is likely to be excessive and unrealistic, neglecting to recognize relationships or the principle of cause and effect. It represents—as it should—your inner Child's dreams and fantasies.

Your second list, by comparison, has undergone dramatic changes. Your "ideal adult" has automatically taken command. The revised list is shorter, more specific and realistic, more *adult*. You have discovered that if one particular need is met, many others will follow logically. The emphasis has shifted unconsciously from demands on the world outside yourself to an inner concern. One desire now leads reasonably to the next—so much so that the first two or three items on your second list, once achieved, might well embrace or include all those remaining.

RECONCILING THE REAL AND THE IDEAL

With the revised list before you, begin a two-chair dialogue with your concept of the "ideal adult." Picture that "ideal person" clearly in your mind, because it represents what might be termed your Future Adult. Give it a name, *your* name, and talk directly to it about what you have discovered as the qualities most important to you, the Current Adult, for successful living. Assume that this

Future Adult is your closest friend, able and willing to listen and understand your views. Read the list aloud, clarifying why the items listed are in that order, explaining also how each of them will bring you the life you have always wanted. Finally, ask that Future Adult to discuss each entry on your list with you, agreeing or disagreeing as to its position, and suggesting whether or not any item might be added or removed.

Now, change places and talk to the Current Adult, the person as you are this moment, in the other chair. Try to evaluate your list from this new point of view. Honestly attempt to offer praise where a right choice suggests it, as well as suggesting constructive criticism and possibilities for revision. "I like the awareness that led you to put health and happiness at the top of your revised list, Mary," your Future Adult might say, "but exactly how does happiness differ from inner peace? Maybe happiness isn't possible *without* inner peace, so wouldn't it be wiser to interchange them on the list and see if that makes more sense?" Change places again, if necessary, and defend your Current Adult's hierarchy of values if you feel you should, but always allow your Future Adult to answer. Have an enthusiastic dialogue with this Future Adult of yours, and continue it until you both agree the revised list is complete and in proper sequence. Rewrite it if necessary.

When agreement is truly achieved, read the list aloud once again to your Future Adult and ask for final approval. When you have gained this approval, you now have the right to ask, "How did *you* achieve all these things I want so much?" Change places and listen to the response as you play the role of your Future Adult. "Well, Mary," it might respond, "it didn't happen overnight, and the way I got where I am isn't the way everybody does it, but I'll be glad to tell you the way it was with me." Get the dialogue underway by praising your Future Adult for having achieved the accomplishments you are discussing. Take them one by one and listen to what your Future Adult has to say. Change roles freely and ask your Future Adult to explain more fully, or challenge the validity of any statement. If the answer does not seem adequate to you, ask further how your Future Adult can counsel you to achieve a particular goal.

Remember that your Future Adult is your ideal. Your Future Adult is always there with you to help immediately whenever you ask. It is part of you, and you are becoming it.

ACHIEVING INNER UNITY

Once differences between the two parts of you are resolved, sit down with your Future Adult and begin to build a stronger relationship between it and your current self. Discuss the anxieties and frustrations of the day, or perhaps explain an argument you had recently. Ask for advice. Be totally open, knowing that your Future Adult could never betray you. If you envy your Future Adult, it will only smile and say, "Come on! I made it, so why can't you?" Frown back and express your doubts and fears, and answer, "Sure, that's easy for you to say. You didn't just lose your job, and you don't have all these bills to pay. Your husband didn't just leave you. You don't know how *hard* life is!"

"I don't? Well, tell me about it."

"You don't have any idea what I'm going through, or what my childhood was. It's been uphill all the way, and your smug self-confidence doesn't help me one bit!"

"I'm not smug; not really. I'm simply what you'll become some day."

"Let's not pretend any longer . . . I'll never make it!"

"No. Not with that attitude you won't"

"Look, that was a great list of ideal goals we talked about, but let's face facts—I'm a loser."

"How did you decide that?"

"I guess I've known it all along. I knew it way back when I was a child. I've always failed at everything, and all along my parents told me so, and so did everyone else."

"Now, let me get this straight: you say you failed at being an adequate adult when you were a child. Right?"

"Right."

"And so now you feel that you can't succeed as an adult, even though you've long since *become* an adult? I don't think you're being completely fair or honest."

"Well, if you knew my parents you'd understand. I couldn't win."

"You seem to be saying that you're still that child, still dealing with those parents."

"In a way, yes. If you really knew those parents of mine, and what they did to me as a child, you'd see how rough it was."

"Well then, since they're so close, why not introduce me?"

"But—"

"Listen! I'm on *your* side! If I'm going to help as you asked, I have to know everything. Trust me. Have I ever let you down before?"

"Well, no."

"Then why should I start now?"

"But, they're long gone. They're just a part of my past."

"Not according to what you've just been saying. They're right here, right now, so why not bring them in? Let's all of us talk about it . . ."

Go to the door and admit them. Invite them in to meet your Future Adult. It genuinely wants to get acquainted. Assign everyone a place to sit: the Child, the Parent(s), the Current Adult, and your new friend, the Future Adult.

Make introductions all around. See the scene unfolding as clearly as if it were a story on television. Change seats in order to play each role if necessary in the beginning, but most importantly, allow each of them to fully disclose and express themselves. Listen to how each of them attempts intercommunication. Whenever possible, become a member of the viewing audience as they talk among themselves. Often, however, you will be drawn back into the conversation. Participate in the dialogue as you feel now, remembering always that in this easy scene you are primarily a listener, rather than a major participant. Listen actively. What does your inner Child reveal? How does your inner Parent describe and discuss you? What are the reactions and responses of your Future Adult? How do you—your Current Adult—react to these three? Let them all talk as long as they like. Ask questions. Listen to the ensuing discussion. Could it be that *all* of them—not only your Future Adult—that *all* of them, after all, are on your side? If you doubt this, ask them. Have it out. Here, together at last, you have your inner family. Remember, all these facets rage within you on a daily basis. You are trying to sort them out and look at each in its proper perspective. How do these old messages and responses affect your life and your relationship with yourself and others? This dialogue is extremely helpful in clarifying the source(s) and validity of your responses to daily living situations. Instead of acting out of habit, you can now examine the assumptions your reactions are based upon—where did these assumptions come from, are they still valid or useful, do you really need old admonitions anymore? Through positive dialogue like this, you will get to the root of these questions and come to know *your own* self better.

Finally, bring out the list of values that you and your true ally, your Future Adult, have discussed. Ask for everyone's opinion and approval.

Self-Acceptance 2

Once you develop self-awareness, and feel you really know yourself, you are ready to return to the question of self-acceptance. In the next stage of your personal development (a stage I have called Self-Acceptance 2) you reevaluate all you have become aware of, and accept yourself as you are. Later, if you wish, you may also make a decision to change things you do not like.

Self-acceptance involves approaching all problems with a kind of eagerness to greet them (an attitude that virtually insures success). Why not say to a problem, "You exist, but so what? Did you think you were stronger than I am? I am here to solve you!" Problems exist endlessly, but not as threats. Rather, they exist as challenges. They are forever a part of living. Better yet, they are positive proof of our essential being, proof of our ability to feel, to love, to suffer, to relate, and most especially, they are proof of our potential to grow.

For now, consider adopting and thoroughly accepting this basic but challenging attitude: *It is all up to me, and I know it!* It is an absolute prerequisite, however, to feel through your personal experience that you have *already* succeeded in life, that you do not need to be *more* happy. If that "more" should happen, it is simply an attractive addition to your completeness. Meantime, you need not work inordinately hard to achieve anything. You need not kill yourself in the process of trying unnecessarily hard to "make it," to succeed, to be happy—not if you finally admit that it is already true. You are a great person—just as you are!

Self-Image

Let us begin by taking a closer look at this so-called "mysterious inner self." Whether you are fifteen, twenty-five, forty, or seventy, you have an internal image of who and what you believe yourself to be. You think you have a knowledge of what you have missed in life, and a feeling about whether or not you can still accomplish what you feel you have missed; and you also have some commitment to the idea that you are a Winner or a Loser.

You were conditioned to believe early in life through parents, relatives, and others that you were clever, attractive, intelligent, or that you were not. If you have a brother or sister, you may have heard countless comparisons about how much better they are in one way or another. Perhaps you have repeatedly heard the compliment, "She's attractive, he's popular, but you're the smart one." This assessment, in time, becomes something like a tape recording or a script; you hear it so often, you eventually come to accept it as absolute truth.

The damage involved in keeping a false image (the result of negative input) is sometimes so deep you may need a will of iron to even look at childhood photographs, facing them only to experience again that painful repetition of unpleasant comments.

A note of caution: be unafraid of living temporarily in any fantasy world. You have, in fact, endless fantasy worlds already within your grasp from which to choose. You may already be living in one of them; perhaps, unfortunately, you have taken up permanent residence there. Being unaware of this fact, clearly, is not to your advantage. Even fantasy worlds and dreams have their limits and their limitations.

To move from one fantasy world to another, once you have found the directional switch, is as easy as changing channels on your television set. The ability to fantasize is a rich gift, but like all gifts, it must be used with proper authority and gratitude. You have the intrinsic right and the fundamental ability to fantasize. Perhaps even without knowing it, you have used this gift all your life. In a dentist's chair you have put yourself ahead in time to enjoy the pleasant evening ahead. During a boring concert or lecture you may have dreamed of lying in the embrace of the one you love. In the darkest moment of a crisis you have pictured yourself in a far-off timeless land, totally free from responsibility, guilt, or obligation.

"You're a dreamer," the world around you seems to say, and you are fully aware people mean this as no compliment. The world seems to distrust dreamers; it seems to disapprove, especially if the dreamer is wide awake.

This assessment is, however, incorrect and unfair. All people dream, they all fantasize, and they all escape in time into their own private worlds. Fantasy is essential for every person's equilibrium, as well as a major source of insight. It is a process to be trusted entirely. But it has its price tag. You must always remember where your dreams and fantasies end, and where your current existential reality begins.

Seeing Through New Eyes

As you examine your self-image, reconsider the past. As if you had never seen them before in your life, look again at those old photographs, especially the ones in your head. Accept them all. Find the charm and attractiveness inherent in them as if you were browsing through the family album of your closest friend. Look penetratingly at each picture, together with a will to enjoy the many *good* memories they hold, and the endless positive implications they hold. Then, begin an entirely new dialogue with yourself, about yourself: "Isn't this a beautiful baby!" or, "Here's an attractive teen-ager!" and, "I like this person!" Then you might add, "Not perfect, no; but then, who is? How very fortunate to have been born at all, and especially being born as such an important and worthwhile human being. Look into those eyes; you can see it all right there. . . !" Become acquainted with yourself and your past in a new and positive way.

Look inward, moving about freely in time and space, and acknowledge that you have this choice: "I can now give myself the permission, the power, and the self-assertiveness to re-experience myself all over again from the very day of my birth, and I can learn to love myself completely. I am *my* child now, and also my best friend. Many people in the past may not always have treated me fairly, but nevertheless, I choose now to be a loving parent to myself—the ideal kind of parent, loving and gentle with myself.

REWRITING THE SCRIPT OF CHILDHOOD

Experience again how warm and good it feels to be cuddled and embraced, and to hear "I love you. . . !" Practice it consciously, and repeat it as many times as needed to experience the total self-acceptance of that tender, lovable child within you. That child is still inside you, waiting for you somewhere in the past, still very hungry for the positive, joyful experience of your full acceptance. Have a warm and friendly dialogue with your inner child, and entice that timid little fawn out into the open. Let your inner child know, through your new experience, that you were (and are!) just as beautiful, just as kind, and just as smart as those you may have been unfavorably compared to (or compared yourself to) in the past.

Accept yourself now as a success, and that is literally all that it takes. Is it truly that simple? "No . . . that's impossible" you say. *Yes; it is truly that simple.* Try it before you judge. Experience never lies.

Take a mental journey, and re-live your life as far back as you can remember. Recall all the fun, all the excitement, all the joy, all those genuinely good experiences you had when no one was watching. You played, you pretended, and all of it was safe. It is still safe, the joy is still there— unless you have changed it, unless you have bolted the door against that joy by thinking, "It's stupid of me to be wasting my time playing games like this at my age!" What logical reason is there to lock out that joy? Remember chasing butterflies? Watching clouds as they moved? Seeing dreams and pictures floating by? Lying on your back in the tall grass? "Wasting time" rather than reading that book or doing your homework?—and all because no one could find you to frown and pass judgment. You were free then. You can claim that same freedom again. It's yours for the taking.

RE-EXPERIENCING THE PERSON YOU WERE AND STILL ARE

Go away *alone* to one of those scenes you nostalgically associate with childhood: ambling along a restful beach with its rolling surf, sitting in a quiet green mountain meadow, dozing aimlessly under a tree, wading through a brook, watching slow-eyed cattle graze, picking wild flowers, following the sunset flight of birds. Re-live all those experiences, and return again to those delicious fantasies and games you once could enjoy without guilt, without feeling bad or guilty.

Take your time. Assume it is the most important day of your life, and that all of it was made especially for you. Take off a day from work if the weekend hours are committed to other things. Say to yourself: "Here is happiness once again. Here is where I left the experience of accepting myself, of truly being myself, of enjoying all those crazy, lazy things in my head, basking in every beautiful moment of it." Accept this child within you that has been denied acceptance for all these years, denied its basic pleasures —pleasures withheld simply because they were not *goal-oriented*. Accept this child now.

The thrill of being both the child and the adult at the same time, of allowing the child and the adult within you to be the best of friends and on the best of terms, is an extremely rewarding experience. If you can come to experience this, then you are a happy individual. You have *"made it;"* and you know it was worth all the effort to try.

Your Parents and the Child-Adult Unity Within You

Whether you are a parent or hope to become a parent, whether you defy or deny parents, you are nonetheless a product of parenthood—the result of a physical union of a man and woman. Biologically, the closest people to your self as you now possess it are your parents. You must reconcile yourself to the fact that your parents are an inescapable part of you. Good or bad, you cannot ignore the fact that you have to deal with your feelings toward them, as well as experiencing and understanding them. Only then can the inner unity of the child and adult within you be complete.

Most parents want their children, but many genuinely do not. Before the discovery of the pill, parents were far less capable of planning the arrival of their children. Most of us, in that sense, are accidents—and yet we were accepted and loved. An important fact emerges, the fact that most young adults are, or were, in fact not adequately prepared for the demanding role of parenthood. They may be emotionally unprepared, still dealing with their own specific maturity. They may be materialistically unprepared, not yet able comfortably to afford their offspring. And they may be psychologically unprepared, not yet having achieved their personal life goals, completing their education, acquiring a profession, or stabilizing their own intimate and immediate relationships. Your parents, too, probably went through these problems.

Parents make mistakes because they are fallible human beings, and in many cases they are not even consciously aware of those mistakes. At times a child can become a kind of scapegoat, blamed by its parents for their unhappiness, their frustrations, for their sense of failure. Perhaps completely unaware, parents can play this self-defeating game with themselves. They decide that they could be happy if it were not for their children. They had to be suffering to be driven to such a conclusion, and as a result, their children suffered as well. Parents are not (nor have they ever been) perfect. Realizing and accepting this will go a long way toward helping you to better understand them.

Complete child-adult unity remains unachieved until both the child and the adult within us can look back and be willing, despite the anger and hurt, to remember, re-experience, and re-evaluate. A forthright decision to be fair with yourself and your parents will lead you back easily to those many gentle and tender moments in the past. Remember how mother dressed you, or how she told you a bedtime story, how father played ball with you, or how his laughter rang out in fun. Visualize everything clearly and re-experience all the happiness and closeness you so often felt toward both your parents then.

The Bridge Between Child and Adult Within You

Tradition teaches us, "Respect and honor your parents, and obey your elders." Some contemporary philosophies, however, counter with "It is all their fault, so you have a right to hate your parents, to express that hatred, to even forget that they are your parents. You owe them nothing; deny your feelings. Had it not been for their cruel irresponsibility, you would be well-adjusted and happy." But what illogical nonsense it is to feel torn between these two extremes (and they *are* extremes), or to deny the one aspect and embrace the other. You might as well insist there is only day without night, or only night without day.

The umbilical cord physically connecting you to your mother and psychologically connecting you to both your parents is cut three times. The first is at birth, a biological severing of infant from mother. This is the time when you experience separation and the beginning of your own individuality or oneness. You have become a separate and unique being, symbolically being *named* by your parents (an act which might well be termed the first of many impositions made on you by others). As well, you are defined as male or female with all the role expectations, behavior, and personality to accompany that label. Here is the first duality you may have discovered in the complex process of achieving your own identity—you find yourself unique and alone, and yet you have also been defined and are expected to behave in a specified manner as a certain type of human being.

The second severing of the umbilical cord is during the rebellious and self-assertive years of puberty, the teen-age years. Sexual maturation brings with it an enormous surge of power. It is then you discover yourself all over again, your new strength, your power to disagree, to express opinions, to make demands. You also realize more clearly the interdependency of your family, and the need your parents have of *your* love and affection, and you realize the impact of your overt expressions of anger, disrespect, disobedience, sense of power, the effects of your psychological and/or physical distance. You assert your independence and examine your power. The question of who is in control becomes a continuous battle. Some people never grow out of this rebellious stage, and therefore never discover the inner peace and happiness that accompanies the loving and accepting of parents in a healthy, happy child-adult unity.

They lose, and so do their parents. These rebellious individuals lose one of life's deepest and most tender joys—the ability to give and receive genuine love. They are usually people who are forever unable to create deep and lasting relationships with others. The unresolved anger from their childhood conflicts with their parents is retained and projected onto others, whether they be lovers, friends, marriage partners, or their own children.

The following three exercises will guide you in resolving any remaining inner conflicts you still might have about your own parents. These exercises will help you be aware of the parent within you, as well as offering insight into how you can present your own child with more positive self-love experiences.

Loving your parents, and letting them know you love them through the child-adult unity within you will make you a stronger and happier person, as well as a more mature adult who can integrate positive parenthood into current activities. These exercises can also be useful in understanding your life cycle experiences more completely.

RE-EXPERIENCING A POSITIVE RELATIONSHIP WITH PARENTS

Write down all the good times you have had with your mother, but avoid creating any hierarchy, a degree of importance or value attached to any of these experiences. They could be as simple as going to the market with her to buy something you wanted, telling her a secret, or helping her cook in the kitchen. Similarly, recall the positive times with your father, remembering even the smallest experience. Perhaps it was simply being with him, a pleasant meal or holiday, or a special outing with him. Allow yourself to feel these memories deeply. If your parents are alive and near you, openly recall these experiences, sharing them with these two very important people. Nothing will please them more than realizing that your past happiness is still alive. If they are far away, write to them. Discuss those pleasant moments with your partner as well, your friends, or your own children. Reinforce the feeling of how good it was, and still is, just to be alive, to be able to relate, to experience, and to enjoy.

Now, change roles, and play each of your parent's parts. See mother's face, her loving eyes. Try to recall again what she wore, and exactly where that good experience took place, which city, which street, which room. Become the child who can express in adult language the feelings of how wonderful it was for mother and father to give you all those delightful treats. Try to use their language. Play the roles back and forth, first being your parent, then being you.

RE-EXPERIENCING NEGATIVE EXPERIENCES WITH PARENTS

Let yourself get in touch with hurt and pain again. Time has mellowed you; it has made you far more capable of facing faded abuses from the past than you might imagine. Write down all the painful experiences as they enter your consciousness, again with no hierarchy or value judgement. If you were punished by being sent away from the dinner table, if you were struck by one of your parents, if you felt a brother or sister got more attention than they deserved, or that you were deprived of something you wanted very much, then express your feelings to that parent in a Gestalt method. Talk to each of them separately, as if they were there in the room with you right now.

"Mother, remember when I was eight years old?" you might begin. "Do you remember how you locked me in my room, and just because_____? I cried and begged you to let me out, but you didn't listen. I hated you! Yes, I hated you so much. . . . Why did you do it, Mother?" Experience all the pain once more. Be eight years old again, with those same feelings.

Now, play mother's role, and express her feelings. Play both roles simultaneously.

Do the same with your father. Don't be afraid to express all the hostile, hateful feelings you had. Now, change places again, and present his side of the story to yourself. Maybe you will begin to feel he had legitimate reasons after all.

RE-EXPERIENCING YOUR PHYSICAL DEPARTURE

The third severing of the umbilical cord, like the second, is symbolic rather than physical. Go back and experience again the emotion-packed scene of leaving home. All parties concerned, most particularly you, had very mixed feelings. Almost like the physical act of birth itself, you were leaving protection and familiarity behind, entering a mysterious new future full of threats and promises. See the faces in that scene, most definitely including your own, and listen to the words again. It was a time when feelings ran so deep that words were meaningless. Re-experience those deep feelings. Cast yourself in the other roles, too. Feel how they must have felt; say what they tried to say. If there were tears, see them shed again.

Re-experience and reaffirm how difficult it was to merge the threat of fear and sadness in leaving home with the promise of excitement and adventure ahead. Feel first one, and then the other, see-sawing back and forth, just as it was back then. Even now there are times when you long

to go back and be that child again. "But that's impossible,"
you say. *No, it is not!* You have been doing it periodically
all of your adult life. The only new thing you have learned
is that you can admit to it.

Self-Esteem 2

I have always liked Virginia Satir's summary of self-
esteem.* I think she captures its basic elements very well
when she writes that self-worth easily flows with feelings
of integrity, honesty, responsibility, compassion and love.
A person with good self-esteem feels that he matters, has
faith in his own competence, is able to ask others for help
while believing he can make his own decisions and is his
own best resource, doesn't have rules against anything he
feels, and accepts all of himself as human. Conversely,
Satir points out, low self-esteem locks a person into distrust, loneliness and isolation to the extent he becomes
apathetic and indifferent towards himself and those
around him. Generally, our feelings of self-esteem,
whether low or high, are learned in childhood. If, as a
child, your parents taught you to have very good feelings
about yourself, you are fortunate indeed. However, if you
entered adulthood with a low estimate of your personal
worth, you have suffered needlessly—but you need not
suffer endlessly. A sense of self-worth, a comfortable feeling of self-esteem, can be honestly built. You need only
take the responsibility for doing so. Only *you* can.

At this point, you should have a sense of confidence
that you know yourself and that you accept yourself
('cause baby, you're what you've got!). Now you must
respect yourself as the agent responsible for making your
life happy. You must build the self-loving and self-

*_Peoplemaking_ by Virginia Satir, Science and Behavior Books, Palo Alto,
1972, p. 22.

indulging part of you, because *you* have to care enough for yourself to see to it that you are happy. This is the core of self-esteem: feeling (and *knowing*) you deserve to be happy.

DISCLOSURE OF DESIRE AND RESOLUTIONS

Whenever a person considers self-esteem, resolutions will soon appear. Sit down and list them as they come to you. Such self-disclosure will point out areas you would prefer changed. Your list might begin like this:

1. I truly love my parents, and I'll try to understand and accept the mistakes they made earlier. After all, they had their own problems.

2. I've experienced some of the fears and pain of my childhood again, but I'm an adult now and I can live with it.

3. I want my parents to know I love them, that I no longer expect them to be perfect. Like me, they are human and imperfect. I can finally see that. I'll tell them.

4. I want *all* the members of my family to see that I have grown to the point that I admit I have been unfair to hate them for what is history.

5. I want the pleasure of accepting my family and of seeing them happy in my love for them. I'll tell them so.

6. I realize now that I don't have to keep proving over and over who or what I am, or how good I am at my work. I already have that proof. The people I work with accept me; what more could I ask?

7. Instead of worrying about "keeping what I have," I want to channel my energies into enjoying things I love to do, or have always wanted to do.

8. I've always wanted to try new and fascinating things in life I've never dared try before: to ski, to dance well, to write, to paint, to sing, to redecorate a room, to study law,

to work with leather, to make a rug, to play the guitar. *Just
think of all the things in life I haven't done yet!* Scuba diving,
belly dancing, inventing something, rowing a boat, sculpt-
ing the perfect body in clay, photography, building furni-
ture, gardening, cooking. What an exciting world to live
in, a world I've shut myself out of all these years! I could
list a hundred things I could do, things I've always wanted
to try!

Make a list of your own resolutions, and then communicate your feelings to someone you are close to. Tell them
about who you are now and how you want to change. The
first purpose in affirming this aloud is for you to listen
again to your inner experiences, the discovery of who you
are, and what you *could* be. A second reason is that verbalizing will help you *accept and love* yourself, in spite of
(and because of) the crazy mixture of positive and negative
feelings you carry within you (just as every human being
does). The third, and perhaps most important, reason to
write and talk about your new horizons is that this will
lead you to specific and concrete plans concerning what
areas you would like to change, and exactly how to go
about it. When you arrive at this point, you should write it
all into a Personal Commitment Contract. The basic and
supreme goal involved in writing such a contract with
yourself is that it marks the beginning of your personal
decision and commitment to achieve what all human beings desire: to become more content, more self-fulfilling,
more at peace with the person you love most, the person
you must spend the rest of your life with—*you*.

A Personal Commitment Contract

I believe in contracts. Freely commit yourself to what you
feel as of now are goals worthy of pursuit. If the Current
You has sufficient desire, capability, and motivation to

attain anything for the Future You, no obstacle will prove too great.

Personal Commitment Contracts are written to be broken. They can be changed, elaborated upon, parts deleted or totally rewritten at any time in the future. "Why write one at all," you might well ask, "if I know in advance I won't fulfill it!" The answer is simple. *You* are changing constantly. The Current You is daily evolving into the Future You. Within the hour you could learn something, meet someone, experience a decision to alter the entire course of your life. You are also human, very capable of error, but you are free and alive and constantly interacting with the changing world around you. To succeed, you must remain flexible. To feel obligated to obey yesterday's contract despite the arrival of new circumstances would be unwisely rigid, imprisoning yourself with decisions made at a time when many factors had not yet become known.

"Don't start anything you can't finish," our parents have cautioned us all. Here again, implicitly this time, is the annoying word "should." Those old parental commands of what we "should" and "shouldn't" do are still with us. Left unchanged, any contract we make with ourselves might easily fall into the same category. You are no longer a child to be enslaved by a contract telling you what you "should" do; far better to have one telling you what you *could* do. A vast difference lies between "I should be happy" and "I could be happy!" You are an adult now, and you have set your inner child free from all those commands. That free child has been integrated into an open and equal partnership with your free inner parent. You are strong and complete as an adult now, not bound by those old inhibiting and constraining "shoulds." If not, it is time for a child-parent conference, an inner dialogue to make certain the Current You and Future You are in command, and no longer only the child or only the parent part of you.

The contract you are about to write with yourself is

based on all the experiences and exercises you have encountered up to this point in your life and in this book. To prepare further, ask yourself a series of searching and penetrating questions before you attempt to write your contract. What is my life actually all about? What do I really want? Each person has not only the right but the boundless ability and obligation to be his own philosopher. No one can give personal meaning to your life but you. No one but you can completely answer your questions. What is meaningful in life to you? What is worthwhile enough for your time? Where do you honestly want to be involved?

FANTASY FUTURES—TRYING THEM ON FOR SIZE

In your search to discover true personal values, ask yourself the following questions. Experience each of these situations as if it had just happened. After careful consideration, write down two or three brief responses to each of these fantasy futures.

1. You have just received an anonymous gift of ten million dollars. Is your future now secure? If not, what else would you need to feel total security? If the answer is yes, how do you intend to spend the money, and what will happen with the rest of your life?

2. You have just received the gift of a Ticket to Freedom. Define freedom; exactly what does the word mean to you? How do you feel now that you have this ticket? Notice that the ticket has an expiration date. What would you do with it if it expired in twenty-four hours? in thirty days? in one year? in twenty years?

3. You have just received permission to retire early from the old "rat race" of goals to achieve and ladders to climb. You may now seek out only positive experiences that could bring you pleasure, inner peace, satisfaction, ex-

citement, and joy. What would you seek out? Assume you are speeding along Achievement Avenue when this happens, hurrying on toward Success Boulevard. Give the wheel to your Future Self, and begin a dialogue. Where would your Current Self say to go? Where would your Future Self suggest? Should you get off the thoroughfare? What about other routes, the ones waiting within you? Have you covered every possible course so that your choice will be a wise one? Down Satisfaction Lane, along Peacefulness Place, over Aliveness Road, and did you notice that "For Sale" sign on Happiness Way? Ask your Future Self what turns you should take to get you there now. Ask for specific directions about how to shift the style and pace of your life. What if your Future Self should pull over and park? Would you get out and walk? What pathway would you take? Where would that pathway lead?

4. You have just been granted the right to be your own best friend. You need never again feel alone. You now have the right to love yourself fully. Boredom is a thing of the past. You are now free to laugh, cry, give, receive, relate, experience and appreciate all the joys of mutual experience. How would that change your future? What would you and your best friend decide to do?

5. You have just been elected president of "Me, Incorporated." You are now presiding over an important meeting of the board. Each day of your life, past and future, has one vote. What would be the items on your agenda? How many votes would be cast for each of your proposals?

WRITING YOUR PERSONAL COMMITMENT CONTRACT
ME, INC.

Date: _____

Place: _____

Personal Commitment Contract

of _____

WHEREAS:
I like my Current Self for the following major reasons:*

a)_____

b)_____

c)_____
AND WHEREAS:
I dislike my Current Self for the following major reasons:

a)_____

b)_____

c)_____

---
*This list is one to be emphasized. Should you reach the end of the alphabet, continue on with: aa), bb), cc), etc.

THEREFORE, LET IT BE KNOWN:
The following is entered in proof that I am eager and able to begin further improvements today. Below listed are changes that have *already* been achieved within me, such productive changes that I am willing to build upon them toward my own greater personal happiness:

a)_____

b)_____

c)_____

THEREFORE, LET IT FURTHER BE KNOWN:
I now know how to change at a greatly accelerated pace, how to improve, how to enhance life and my enjoyment of it, and I intend to begin more fully becoming my Future Self by the following steps:
a) I acknowledge my love of life itself, and I know that I am free to accept it, free to live it, free to make it as full and enjoyable as possible for myself and for others. I deserve it. They deserve it.
b) I love the discovery that I am a necessary and important part of life, that I truly am the master of myself, that my personal life style belongs solely to me, engaged as I am toward the ultimate fulfillment I desire in order to take my rightful place in the world.
c) I also acknowledge that among my many gifts is the freedom to choose my own friends, my own activities, my own time alone, my own time with others.
d) I love my parents, and I intend to remind them of it continually in order that they be certain that I truly accept them for what they are.
e) I love_____, my closest partner in life, and I intend to tell him/her now and in the future, so I will be certain that he/she knows I truly accept them for what they are.
f) I love my children, and I intend to remind them con-

tinually so they will be certain I truly accept them for what they are.

g) I love the following people who have enriched my life, and I intend to continually communicate my gratitude for their existence:

1. _____

2. _____

3. _____

h) I love the following activities in my life, and I intend to show my appreciation for them by engaging in them more fully:*

1. _____

2. _____

3. _____

i) I love the following "simple" pleasures of merely being alive, and I intend to show my appreciation by enjoying them to the fullest extent possible:*

1. _____

2. _____

3. _____

THEREFORE, LET IT BE RESOLVED:

a) I commit myself to the conditions and reservations of this contract to the utmost of my present abilities.

b) I declare that the above statements are the whole truth

*These lists could be virtually endless, so try to limit them to a reasonable number.

as honestly set forth at this time to best of my ability.
c) I reserve the right to re-examine, revise, and alter this contract whenever and however deemed necessary or expedient to the undersigned.
d) I further promise to re-examine, reconsider, and/or re-establish the above statements at reasonably spaced intervals, changing, improving, and revising any entries herein which are no longer applicable, as well as reaffirming my commitment to whatsoever I have herein stated as fact.

HEREUNTO SWORN BY MY HAND THIS DATE

_____
(Date)

_____
(Signature)

Once completed, your *Personal Commitment Contract* may be filed away with other important papers and documents. It would be wise to put it in a place where it may be readily referred to, and yet not be available to easy discovery. It is an extremely personal document, not meant for other eyes. Before putting it away, read the entire document again, making certain it is truly a genuine reflection of your insight and commitment. Decide for yourself specifically when you should re-examine it for appraisal and re-evaluation—in the full knowledge, of course, that it must grow, change, and be altered as you yourself evolve. Monthly or bi-monthly re-evaluation might be advisable at this time.

You are now ready to communicate to others. You have been through a difficult but rewarding experience, a process that entitles you to attempt totally effective communication. You have, after all, achieved the most effective communication of all—the disclosure of your self to yourself.

Self-Assertiveness:

Self-assertiveness follows self-esteem. Self-esteem leads you to the conclusion that you deserve to give yourself those things you need in order to be happy. Self-assertiveness is the action component; it is the reaching out to attain those goals, reaching out for the things needed for happiness.

Assertiveness is different from aggressiveness. It is also a "loaded" word when applied to women. In our culture, an assertive man is masculine, strong, successful; but to call a woman assertive has usually implied she is pushy, aggressive, bitchy, masculine—definitely not a lady. Of course, all this is in the process of change, and women are asserting their right(!) to assertiveness.

Aggressiveness is linked with manipulative behavior; with the old idea that the end justifies the means, that if you think you're justified, you can do anything. By subscribing to this philosophy you are using others, hurting them, and exploiting them.

Assertiveness is simply the behavior based on valuing yourself enough to insist on getting what you want and need by using reasonable and fair means.

Using "I-Messages"

As a first step, concentrate on using "I-messages" to clarify your goals. Don't say "I must," "I should," or "I have to." These put the source of action outside yourself. These are not true I-messages. They are other-messages—something (or somebody) other than you is making you do this. Try to clarify your goals by working out a statement of the situation which avoids such terms. For example, you might have been telling yourself, "I have to visit my mother very often." Try working that around. It might go something like this: "I don't really want to visit my mother, and there is very little pleasure for me in doing so. She is sick, and it is depressing to sit with her." Then you might go on, "But I want her to know I love her, and so I really want to do this—even though there is little immediate pleasure for me in the visit itself." Now you have clarified your goal—and it is *your* goal. Or, depending on the situation, it might turn out as follows: "I really don't have to visit so often—her needs are taken care of without my presence, and I would probably be a better visitor if I went less often and really made it special when I did go. So, I'll compromise; I won't visit so often. But I do want to visit her sometimes, because I love her, and when I do, I will work to make it special so both she and I will really enjoy it." Again, you have clarified what you want—you have asserted your needs and desires.

Self-assertiveness also involves working out strategies to obtain what you want. Notice that part of self-assertiveness is clarification of goals, part is planning to achieve them, and part is acting to carry out your plans. The key is to plan alternative strategies for achieving what you need. Always have options and alternatives open for use. Then, you will be more likely to attain what you want.

chapter 5

Communication with Self and Others

We live in a world filled with people, a virtually endless variety of threats and promises. How well we approach and share that world is directly influenced by our own inner readiness. How adequately we are prepared and whether we succeed or fail is dependent on how open and communicative we are with ourselves and with others.

Positive self-assertiveness, as well as effective communication, is based on the inner self being revealed. If a person is not familiar with the complexity of his inner self, he can scarcely be expected to assert himself effectively. He does not know how he truly feels, and therefore becomes the unwilling target of inner conflicts.

Communication with Self

Each of us must first come to terms with what exists within. This is a major prerequisite to any success we have in any outward venture we might attempt. Growth begins within and expands outward, and mental growth is no exception. From the seed of increasing self-awareness, we expand and grow to include more and more of what surrounds us. This process demands constant communication with our inner selves. Just as we decide we have achieved our goal of inner unity, a new element appears and we realize we are far from that goal. This inner process of constant expansion and growth is based on acceptance. When that acceptance is suppressed or absent, growth is hampered proportionately. Without self-acceptance, there can be no open channels for inner communication, and the process needed for self-knowledge is blocked. In effect, we limit our ability to grow in direct proportion to the degree we limit our ability to conduct open inner dialogues. The process of communication with self goes on unceasingly, and these dialogues with self are the continuing basis for dialogue with others.

If the basis for effective inner communication is self-acceptance, it is also true that acceptance of others is the basis for communication with them. How you feel about yourself is mirrored in how you feel about others. If you trust yourself, and that trust is based on self-awareness, you will tend to approach others on a trusting basis. The language of success comes from within. If you operate on the basis of a positive self-image, it is all but impossible to achieve negative results.

Communication as Sharing

As we make discoveries about ourselves, we find we have a genuine need to share those discoveries. Each of us is a station or link in a complex system of potential communication. Each of us can send messages as well as receive them, but the unique and challenging aspect in this ability of ours is that both inner and outer change is inevitable. Whether or not that change constitutes personal growth is based on our willingness to be open and receptive.

Human communication is little different from any other form of communication in that it requires a sender and a receiver. When one of these two components is absent, communication will cease. The effect of this can be seen in turning a radio knob to "off." If you think of effective communication as the flow of energy, it is easy to see why openness at both ends is an absolute necessity. If that message is blocked at either point, the transmission cannot be completed.

The need to communicate with others is very different from a need to be dependent. Rather than sharing, a dependent person wants to take, and an imbalance results. On the pretense of sharing, such a person is cloaking his inner lack of security. "Help me!" is the essence of the message. It is the outward demand of someone who has not allowed his inner system of communication to function. Therefore, he must rely on the strength of others. Because of his lack of inner acceptance and self-knowledge, he must depend on substitutes from the outside. He needs constant praise and reassurance from others, the "positive strokes" that Transactional Analysis describes. He is unhappy and unfulfilled when he fails to receive enough positive attention from others. He is dependent on the world, locked at the level of a child operating with his parents. He has not accepted himself, which leads him to the endless search for acceptance from others. Hence, his ability to function is based on what is given him from the outside. He wants medals, trophies, and gold stars as symbols of his worth. He is a person who fails to recognize his own worth, and he must therefore demand others reassure him of it. Marriage or any other relationship is doomed to failure when it is based on the need to depend on the other person, rather than on the need to share. Everyone has experienced a relationship based on dependency. It is a process of taking, as opposed to one of giving. These false unions are predictably brief and unsatisfactory.

The secure person who is capable of sharing is one who has an active inner life. Because of this active inner life he has a need to *share* with others, not a need to *depend* on them. He is pleased with himself, pleased with what he has found in life, and he wants to share it. He is capable of giving as well as receiving. He is searching for exactly the kind of equality in a relationship that a weakened and dependent person cannot tolerate.

Each human being perceives an endless variety of relationships around him. No matter what the age, sex, or station of those involved, effective communication and its principles of sharing based on self-worth does not change. Only when you are willing to confront yourself first, will you find anything to communicate. You can be honest with others only if it is based on a similar honesty with yourself. Part of honesty is a strong sense of responsibility. It is a lack of responsibility that leads the dependent person to ask his listener to take care of him, to think for him, and to make his decisions. He is actually asking others to take responsibility for the success of his life. This is a request that, in the end, will never adequately be fulfilled from the outside.

Self-Responsibility

The primary responsibility we all have is to ourselves. Our responsibilities to partner, parents, children, friends or a job are all based on how responsible we are to our inner selves. No one else can be held accountable for what we are. We must accept and understand our inner selves, and on that basis take full responsibility for our actions. Those who refuse to communicate with their inner selves are terrified at the prospect of total responsibility, and they promptly place it on someone else's shoulders. "She made me do it" and "I had no choice" are common justifications of the refusal to accept the fact that all our decisions are our own.

When we arrive at a decision, we need to check within and decide whether or not the choice is correct. It is not an intellectual process of asking "Why?" since the answer must then begin with "Because. . ." This personal process of checking with our inner selves is concerned with whether or not our choice is truly a correct one for ourselves *specifically*, and if so, to accept the responsibility to carry it out. We are essentially responsible beings, familiar with the fact that accepting responsibility for our choices means understanding the bases on which those choices are made. Inevitably, the cycle leads back to self-awareness. What decision is right involves dealing with what *feels* right. Discovering what feels right is not the process of the "why—because" formula, but rather a penetrating process of self-exploration. It is not an ethical judgement, it is a personal one. The greater our awareness of self is, the better our choices become.

The responsibility that results from any choice, and our understanding of that choice, constitutes the basis for continued and increased self-communication. This in turn becomes a source of strength, creating increased effectiveness in our communication with others. Humanistic psychology defines such an accomplishment as that of a "self-actualized" person, one who is able to share "peak experiences," "ecstasy," or "meanings and values" with others. When we arrive at this level, we experience an additional aspect of communication, an enthusiasm quite apart from the message given. Although difficult to define, the totality of sharing seems to fall in the area of excitement or joy.

Needs and Risks

The fact that we have a message to communicate does not materialize magically from nowhere. It is the result of a need. That need involves our emotions, and it contains an element of excitement. We have experienced something inwardly, and the need to communicate is a direct result. We must first, of course, understand why that message is significant, what needs we have to fulfill, and then stand ready to assume responsibility for feeling as we do. In addition, we must be willing to communicate the content of that message.

Needs occur on a variety of levels, with differing degrees of intensity. A request to pass the salt is not on as complex a plane as that of a proposal of marriage, but each springs from a need the sender has decided to verbalize. Often the need expressed is simply the result of a desire to share. We all have a variety of needs, and our requests change continuously. Perhaps your need at the moment is for something material (you need to borrow a ladder); or it is a physical need (you require sleep or food); or it could be the need for comfort and emotional support; under other conditions, it could be the intellectual need to gain knowledge.

The expression of need can come from one of two directions. You may have a need to communicate, or someone else may express a need to you. If I communicate my need to you, I expressly hope that you can fulfill it. You are, however, not required to do so; perhaps you are incapable of doing so. Here is where the element of responsibility emerges. It is first my responsibility to express my need, and it is then your responsibility to say how you can respond to that expressed need.

The four variables of communication—content, need, emotion, and excitement—all extract their price from each of us in any form of communication. Sharing them involves taking risks and assuming a responsibility of being precise. This is why elements of courage as well as trust are involved in any process of communication.

Let us imagine that you are planning a trip to Europe, and I have already been there. I want to share some of the experiences about my trip, offering information I feel will enrich your trip. This is the message I intend, the primary element in my communication, but hardly the only one.

What specific needs of mine are being fulfilled in the process? Your need may be simply that of wanting information, but this is not a one-sided contract. In such a process, am I simply sharing and wanting to help make your trip more enjoyable, or am I gaining gratification from the fact I know something you don't, and that makes me feel somehow superior? If I check honestly within myself, I can discover the answer.

An entire range of feelings may be involved in such a dialogue. I may be prompted to recall all manner of negative memories: the anger I felt about a reckless cab driver, the hostility and bitterness involved in a cabaret quarrel, the depression at finding myself alone in a foreign city, or the disappointment of being turned away from a theater. The positive feelings of love and tenderness, of attraction and closeness, of excitement and exhilaration may be equally expressed. We all experience such emotions continuously, and we long to share them with people who are close to us.

In relating my experiences to you, the element of excitement is also likely to appear. This is neither something asked, nor is it consciously given in return. It is nearly on the plane of another language. You cannot predetermine a time, shape, or degree of the exhilarating excitement that can evolve as an unexpected by-product of many conversations. It is an absolutely unpredictable element, most often recognizable in the Gestalt sense, a moment of intensity when you experience that "Ah-ha!" response to awareness.

If you have had a unique and fantastic experience, you may want to attempt to translate it into words and share it with someone. You soon discover, however, that because it is not tangible, this elevation of self is also the most difficult to describe. If you attempt to communicate the joy of sex, or the awe of fully experiencing an orange sunset, the sense of loss death can bring, or the meaning of fulfillment in true love, you are soon led to the awareness that words seem to become inadequate. The moment you attempt description of what Maslow calls a "peak experience," what Carl Rogers terms "ecstasy," what Frankl calls "meanings and values," you then realize this is the least precise area in terms of linguistic concepts. Whenever you approach this kind of sharing, you are confronted with the translation into words of an experience beyond words. The best you can do is to remain close to that experience in your decision to share it with another person. If you say, "I was so impressed with the beauty of that sunset," you realize it is not enough to merely attempt a description. "I wish you had been there with me, to see it too, and to share the excitement," you are soon led to say. Though verbally inexpressible, sharing of this kind is the most intense embrace of life's meaningful experiences.

When you have an experience so beautiful and so big you feel you can enjoy it more if you share it, you have reached a point of excitement that is an act of creation. This is a case where the speaker should be allowed his own fantasy, his own trip through remembered imagery, describing what happened for the sheer pleasure of involving and sharing with the other person. You are saying simply, "I have a beautiful experience to share with you. Just listen and be a part of this because I want the joy of reliving it again with someone close." You may be describing a sunset to the other person, and they will be in touch with the experience through their own visualizing and imagination. Perhaps they will want to share a similar experience.

You have asked me to share, but certainly not to criticize. Criticism is a form of rejection. Responding by saying, "Wasn't it cold sitting out there without a coat? You could have caught a cold," is a highly effective way of destroying your ability and your desire to share. "Wasn't it too late and dangerous to be there? You could have been raped!" would have the same effect. When you are sharing an emotional experience, you are asking merely that it be accepted, and be relived with you.

The end result of such a conversation might well be an invitation for the two of you to share a similar experience together. The excitement of aesthetic joy is difficult to capture. The verbal description is a pale translation of what really happened. Sharing an actual experience is perhaps the most beautiful and most complete way of sharing.

Excitement is also an intrinsic part of the creative process. Conversely, you can say with equal accuracy that the creative process is involved in the element of excitement. Arthur Koestler, in *The Creative Process*, discusses the similar excitement of coming upon an intellectual discovery. When the insight hits you, that is the moment of creation. On whatever level it occurs—sexual, emotional, aesthetic, creative, intellectual—it is the total impact of the experience that consumes you. There do not seem to be enough adjectives in language to describe this level of excitement and awareness. The current slang of the younger generation reflects an attempt to capture this feeling verbally. "Far out!" and "Heavy, man!" are current cousins of former expletives such as "Solid, Jackson!" and "In the groove!"

Rules of Effective Communication

In effective communication between two people, there are basic rules of operation. One person is the sender of a message, the other has the role of the receiver. It is a responsibility of the sender to initiate this process in a self-assertive way. How else can the receiver know the sender has a message unless that fact is verbalized? "Listen, please, because I have something I want to tell you," is an appropriate way to begin (however you phrase it).

The sender's responsibility is to initiate the process by giving a clear signal. In effect, the message says, "I have something to tell you, and I'd like you to listen to me." That message is important, significant because the sender is a worthwhile person. Arriving at the point of saying, "My message is important and urgent," implies that you want to express something at that moment, that you need the undivided attention of the listener, that you respect him sufficiently to truly want him to hear everything. As a sender, it is your responsibility to ask specifically whether or not the other person is ready to listen.

The other person has an equal responsibility: he must respond to the overture before effective communication can properly begin. Perhaps he might say, "I'd like some coffee first," or "Let's go outside under the tree." This response is an attempt to create an appropriate physical environment. Such a listener respects the situation sufficiently to want to make arrangements to give his full attention. This may happen in an off-handed, casual way, but it indicates that even before the process of communication has begun, there are conditions required for the involvement necessary. Both people recognize that these unwritten rules apply to the here and now—not forever—but for as long as communication is to continue. It is a kind of conditional contract indicating that each of us knows we are about to be involved.

The listener has a choice. He can say, "As much as I want to listen to you, I'm not ready now. My attention is somewhere else." His responsibility is to check himself to see whether or not he is capable of giving what the other person asks. Herein lies the element of honesty, and it involves self-awareness. Without this ability, he is being unfair. Both people must agree to this "contract of readiness" before communication begins. Simple as this may sound, failure to express an honest reaction all too often results in ineffective communication. An inner response such as, "Oh no, she's going to start talking and never stop!" when covered by a polite "Yes, I'm ready," is deception. The listener is saying "Yes," and feeling "No."

Why does a person feel one thing and express another? This process of acknowledging readiness is a function many people are totally unaware of. It is usually the result of a lack of genuine self-awareness. Perhaps the listener is secretly frightened at the prospect of confrontation, intimidated, or insecure. An insecure person wants to please, and therefore unconsciously reasons, "If I tell her I'm not ready to listen, she won't like me, so I must give up my impatience and deny its existence." His impatience is the price he feels he must pay for being accepted. This is not an honest response. Each of us owes it to the other person and to himself to be honest when we say, "Yes, I'm ready to listen."

The subject to be under discussion is not the crucial point, but rather the willingness of the listener to respond appropriately. "Where am I in this process?" the listener must reason. "Do I want to receive, or do I want to talk as well?" What happens when one person has a strong need to send you a message, but you have an equally strong need to send a different one? Do you feel strong enough, self-assertive enough to say, "I think my message to you is more important than your message to me"? When needs clash, the people involved are seldom aware of their problem, often resenting one another for unconscious reasons. Perhaps you simply feel that you don't even want to hear a human voice today. If you fail to recognize this or or communicate it, you block the message and its content with your own counter process of resentment. This is why self-awareness and self-disclosure are fundamental to the open flow of effective communication. You must be aware of your feelings before you can attain the conviction to accept or transmit them.

At any point, the listener may become disturbed. He not

only has the right, but he also has the responsibility to say so. Perhaps the speaker is too agressive, too emotional, perhaps repetitive, or too loud. As a responsible listener, you are correct only if you communicate this. "Something is wrong," you should interrupt. "There seems to be a conflicting process happening here, so you'd better stop. I'd like to clarify why I feel this way." If you fail to do this, communication is hampered or stopped. The responsibility of the listener is summoned. He reports that something is interfering with the flow. Until such a point, the speaker has a right to assume that you are listening. He is engaged in his attempt to transmit what he has to say. It is not his responsibility to be concerned over the listener's fluctuating ability to receive.

Each person has a commitment. Listening fully is the listener's concern, and it is also his responsibility to admit it when he is not listening fully. A common cause of the breakdown in communication is the failure of the listener to do precisely this. There are many methods of improving communication, but nothing will suffice if the listener has "tuned you out" and fails to say so. Such dishonesty is often not deliberate; it is simply that the listener is incapable of self-awareness or incapable of asserting himself sufficiently to express it. He may not realize he has left the speaker. He is flooded with thoughts of his own, but keeps this a secret because it is "wrong." The message of the speaker is thereby heard, but not listened to. Meantime, the listener hears that voice increasingly as an interference. Left unchecked, he is soon led to feel that he is a victim, a captive audience being used and manipulated. The energy of the listener is meanwhile being diverted into that inner struggle. He erects defenses, blocking out the message with his personal justifications. A common example is the familiar scene of a husband and wife in combat, and neither is listening. Each person is simply waiting for one to stop long enough for the other to begin.

Effective communication often involves a conscious break. If the listener is aware and honest enough to interject such a confession, he is playing by the rules. "I'd like to listen, but I'm suddenly preoccupied with my mother's illness, and it's blocking my contact with you," he may say. The speaker then has two choices: either to stop the communication until a later time, or to exchange roles and become the listener. "Why don't you go and take care of her, and we'll talk about this another time," you might say, or "What I had to say is important, but it can wait. Let's talk about her."

The roles have been reversed, a new contract thereby formed. Perhaps the other person's need is for help, or merely a similar need to have a listener. Sometimes all that is required is that you can truly say, "I understand. I guess now isn't such a good time for you, so let's stop. I realize you have to see her. Can I be of any help? Is everything all right?" This kind of willingness to exchange roles in itself can often resolve the problem. "Yes, everything is all right. I'm just worried, I suppose. Thanks for listening," could well be the answer. At this point, the checking process is repeated: "Are you sure you're not still concerned about her?" The answer: "No, my mind is clear now. Go on with what you were saying." The shift then may return to the original speaker and listener roles. Whatever the reason may be, once the listener realizes that his part of the contract cannot be kept, he is obligated to report that fact to the speaker. Neither has offended the other. Clarity and honesty are to be feared only when they are neglected.

Life is a continuing process of contracts. As long as those contracts are valid and clear, we have no conflicts. All people have strong needs, but there is no necessity for compromise: out of conflict comes agreement. You want to listen to music, for example, but I want to do something else. We have thereby chosen not to communicate for one evening. Neither resents the other's need, and we go our separate ways. Our contract clearly shows we cannot be on the same level because our needs are different. As long as this is clear, the contract is valid. In this instance, a basic demand of communication between two people has been resolved. They each have clarified their conditions and readiness for communication, finding it temporarily impossible.

Whether speaker or listener, you are neither standing in judgment of the other person, nor are you evaluating him. You are assuming complete responsibility for what you are, for what you feel and know, here and now.

Effective Communication

Effective communication must be in accordance with the truth as you know it at the moment. You must talk in the present tense, first person, and attempt to relate to another person rather than judging him. Your listener has similar responsibilities. He must acknowledge that what you tell him is clear, that your feelings are understood. If not, he needs to check with you as many times as necessary to make certain he has heard what you intended. The best way to check back is simply to repeat what the other person has said, "You're tired and you feel like resting? Did I hear you right?" Checking back with the speaker has a dual purpose. First, it clarifies the message and insures proper interpretation of the message. Second, it aids the other person as well. A good listener encourages the speaker to look deeper within himself.

The human mind involves many layers; there is always something new, some aspect yet undiscovered. The process of communication promotes and encourages trust. The more you trust your listener, the more ready you are to risk looking into the new avenues and depths of your feelings.

As you broaden your awareness and explore new areas

of your self, your exploration takes two directions. Vertical exploration and expression involves exploring a subject to its depths and heights. Horizontal exploration encompasses a variety of related ideas, emotions, and experiences. Communication with others, as well as with self, alternately involves exploration in both directions.

During a conversation, a speaker might elaborate on one thing, going into depths because he feels free and comfortable. Or he may discuss a variety of topics as he is encouraged, not choosing to go into any of them in depth. The listener is creating an atmosphere of trust and encouragement by continuously checking back and asking questions such as, "What else do you see?" or "How do you feel about it? Why don't you tell me more about it." He is thereby giving the speaker the assurance he is truly listening, and helping the speaker to seek out new places in his awareness, urging him to look into the depths of his thinking, as well as allowing him to move horizontally into wider avenues.

This process occurs in all effective communication. The challenge is created by a truly interested and objective listener. It is not appropriate for the listener to attempt to direct or influence the speaker by his outside questions or suggestions. His primary responsibility is to be completely involved in the speaker's message. He does not try to direct or advise, but he encourages by the constant message, "I am with you, listening to everything," and by repeating what he hears, followed by, "Do I hear you correctly?" This is genuine feedback and encouragement, and this is as far as one may legitimately go as an interested listener.

In such interactional communication, the listener does not offer more than the speaker asks. By your questioning the speaker, asking, "How do you feel?" you are encouraging him to look deeper within himself, but you are not being directional. The moment you attempt to direct the speaker, you influence him with your own attitudes, your own subjective thoughts and opinions—thereby guiding rather than listening.

When you manipulate in this manner (however helpful you intend your comments to be), you take away from the speaker what can be termed his "self-responsibility." If you respond by saying you know a better way, or if you offer to advise or guide, you take away that speaker's very important obligation—one he owes to himself. Subjective responses such as criticizing, giving advice, explaining, or attempting to guide are both inappropriate and detrimental. Your function is simply to be there, fully involved, available, and encouraging. Even a sympathetic reaction is incorrect, for a response such as, "Oh, you poor soul!" implies that you can take care of the matter; thus you become the authority figure, the source of strength, again taking away the speaker's "self-responsibility." The speaker is not asking for anyone's strength; he simply wants to share his thoughts with you. By that very sharing you are giving him an important gift, your attention, an attention based on friendship.

In any communication we often shift roles, first becoming the speaker, then the listener. The listener in either case continues to encourage the speaker to look within himself, to assume his own responsibility, thereby helping him to be in closer touch with whatever he is seeking to share. Note this shifting of roles:

Sender: "I'm tense today. I just have too many things on my mind."

Receiver: (first stage of feedback) "Tell me more about it."

Sender: "Perhaps I can get out of it. I don't want to allow so many things to crowd me. I really don't want to be tense."

Receiver: "What else can you tell me about this tension? How do you feel about it?"

Sender: "It's difficult to explain . . ."

New Sender: "You know, when I have too many things to do, I also get tense, but I'm also usually irritable, sometimes even depressed."

New Receiver: "Really? Tell me more about it."

It is important to note, however, that this message from the new sender will be entirely different. What is tension for one is not the same as it is for another.

What if the receiver responds by saying, "It's better to take a walk than to be sad," or, "When you're angry, why don't you hit the wall?" This is giving advice, a response that was not asked for. There are many possible reactions to being sad or angry, but the responsibility for choice of reaction lies within the sender.

If the speaker asks for advice or an opinion, be immediately on guard. There is an enormous difference between telling him your opinion of what you feel he "should" think and relating what you yourself might do in a similar situation. At this point, you have assumed the responsibility of becoming the sender. The key to effective communication is this willingness to assume such a responsibility. Explain what might work for you, but the other person must see that it is not advice. It is, instead, an attempt to share your own subjective views. This still leaves the other person with the responsibility of making his own decision.

Each of us, as a unique individual, behaves and responds to life situations in differing ways. When we make a choice, we cannot project the responsibility for that choice onto anyone else, but we have the right—and the need—to share it. If we choose to try what someone else tells us has worked for him, we must take full responsibility for having made that choice, and for its success or failure.

By being an active, attentive listener, you can encourage the speaker to explore himself in both horizontal and vertical directions. Both the speaker and the listener benefit from the experience. Sharing and exploring with another person is a very rewarding experience. Not only do you both benefit in terms of insight and self-awareness, but you can also take pride and enjoyment in your ability to communicate with another.

Communicating Knowledge

We are cerebral people, and so we enjoy achieving knowledge, and we enjoy categorizing our life experiences in terms of the knowledge we attain. Reading a book, taking a class, traveling—any activity that contains the element of learning—is a rewarding experience. Such a seemingly minor activity as working in our garden affords pleasure on various levels. We enjoy the physical aspect of exerting our energy constructively, we experience aesthetic pleasure in being amid the beauty of flowers and greenery, but the element of knowledge is there as well. If you have planted a fuchsia, by the very act of choosing the plant, you had to learn about it. We operate on many levels, not simply that of emotions, and all these are levels we seek to share. If you want to tell me about your fuchsia, there is more to say than "Isn't it beautiful?" Many other facts surround it, knowledge you have gained that you want to share.

Recent books tend to emphasize that the only important thing is what you feel, ignoring the rest. There is, however, a genuine excitement involved in the precision of communicating knowledge, a very rewarding part of communication. When you are hired for a new job, in another instance, your level of effectiveness is measured in terms of your working knowledge. The people you associate with must bring you up to their level if you are to be an effective worker with them. Communicating sheer knowledge is an important process, both pleasurable and utilitarian, and not one to be underrated.

When we talk about communication in terms of the content of a message, we must be clear about that material, having it ordered in our mind. We must also be aware of the reason we have chosen to communicate it. Avoiding the "why?—because" formula, we should seek to discover what need is being fulfilled. When it is a matter of bragging, of displaying how much more we know than the other person, the message behind the information is that the listener is inferior. Imagine that I wanted to tell you something, my opening comments going something like this: "You mean you don't know about Elizabeth Taylor? Why, it was in all the papers! You mean you didn't read it? I thought *everyone* had heard about it . . . !" Even before the information begins, the message is clear that I consider you inferior. This need of mine to feel superior arises from insecurity, something I need to work out internally. My approach perhaps was not intentional or consciously premeditated, but my inner conflict is immediately apparent. If this is not understood by the one communicating such messages, he will continue to wonder, "Why do I drive people away? After all, I'm so generous in wanting to share myself with them!"

Be aware that no one can possibly know everything in every area. You may very well know many things that I don't. For a long time, for instance, I suffered because I knew little about opera. I felt inadequate, and even ashamed, until I realized that part of self-acceptance is that I am not required to know everything, nor even to have the desire to know everything. If someone opens the subject of opera now, I can guiltlessly respond, "Tell me about it. I know very little."

Whatever the motives, the process of delivering knowledge will not create resentment if we have a clear contract with the other person. An awareness of the process of communicating information is very important. Communication takes place on two levels—the information being conveyed, and the need that prompted the initiation of communication.

We all have a strong motivation to teach others. It is not the distorted need of wanting to talk down to inferiors, but a vital and productive need. In the process of telling others what we know, we are invariably interrupted by questions. Perhaps it is a question we cannot answer. I am always enriched in the process of my attempt to enrich you because you open new avenues. If you fail to understand it all, and you ask me questions, your questions may lead me to realize that I do not understand the subject as well as I thought, or they may inspire me to a deeper understanding of the subject. In this exchange, the sender is as rewarded as the receiver, because it is a process of mutual involvement.

In another instance, let us say that I am interested in photography. When I bring up the subject, I am hopeful of being involved with you on this level. The purpose is growth. I want to share my knowledge, and I want you to share yours. My motivation to communicate is therefore not altruistic, not "good," but I am giving in order to receive. Often without conscious thought, we give because of a feeling the results will be good for us. "What is good for me?" is a question that never ceases to influence our actions. We want gratification, further knowledge, and a stimulus to seek out more. Only through my total acceptance of you—and because that is based on a total acceptance of myself—do you attempt to share knowledge with me.

Self-Disclosure

The element of trust in an exchange or relationship is best attained by self-disclosure. Sum up all the things a person has said to you, and decide whether or not he is capable of accepting himself. If not, he is probably not capable of accepting you. You can promote a new sense of acceptance in him, however, by *your* acceptance. It is then your responsibility to make him aware of your acceptance of him. He will automatically be brought to the conclusion that he can risk doing the same with you. In the effort to grow, yours is the first move. If you do not communicate to him that you accept yourself, he will not be likely to assume that you could accept someone else. When one person takes the initiative, the risk, his listener is brought up short. You have then communicated the unspoken message that you are capable of accepting his inner self as well as you have accepted your own. The most successful marriages, the greatest friendships, are begun on this principle. When this trust and openness occurs, it is best thought of as a discovery that you are not alone in the world. It is a kind of joyful awareness that you and he have each become willing to enter into a relationship in depth, a "mutual conspiracy" from which the rest of the world is excluded.

Sharing means caring. Once that message is conveyed, communication is not the threat it once was. There are many people (and often the least suspected source or in the least suspected places) who are very capable of accepting who and what you are. The "certainty" that there is no one who cares is based on fear. That fear in turn arises from our own unwillingness to accept and communicate—the very prize we seek. Fear of others is often the projected fear of ourselves. If we are unwilling to communicate with all that we are comprised of, there is little we have to offer. We remain ignorant of what we have to offer because we have not yet discovered it in ourselves. We have achieved the ability to communicate with others only to the extent we have achieved the ability to communicate with ourselves.

When you are willing to open yourself to another person, you have done more than exhibit the willingness to be honest—you have created in another person that same willingness. Not in every case will you be successful, but these are certainly not failures. When you first offer yourself as a friend, you cannot know the limits and bounda- ries within the person you seek. Often we conclude that because a person does not respond to us, *we* are therefore the problem. If, however, we present ourselves openly, the problem lies within that other person. The fact that we do not meet his current requirements is his problem, not ours.

It is very easy to assume that because you are rejected by one, you will therefore be accepted by no one. Consider the complexity of your inner life, however, and your achievement of coming into intimate contact with it. You can then realize that those not capable of achieving that inner honesty will view you as a threat to their stability. You are someone willing to be open, and the implicit mes- sage is that you want them to be open with you as well. This often marks the point of breakdown in communica- tion, indicating the other person is unwilling or incapable of handling the situation.

Suggest to a potential friend, "If there is anything you want to know about me, all you have to do is ask." That simple statement creates an explosion of reactions in the listener. Follow it through, and tell that person whatever he wants to know. Be willing to reveal yourself for what you are, and he has only two recourses—he will pursue his interest in what you have to reveal, or he will with- draw. In either case, you have not lost. To communicate to me that you are willing to be real is a threat only if I am not equally willing to reciprocate.

Do not be surprised if such an invitation marks a turn in the conversation. Many people are not at all ready to go beyond the point of communicating the fact that they want you to pass the bread. They want to stay on a "safe" level, talking about their current interests or what was in the paper today. This is a person who has not truly confronted his inner complexity. Despite his other attributes, he is not capable of receiving what you have to offer. He is likely to be dependent and fearful. He may divert the conversation to other matters, disguising the fact that he lives on the surface of life, unwilling and unable to share what either of you is experiencing on a personal level. He is afraid of the relationship because he is afraid of himself. This is not a rejection of you; it is a further rejection of his own inner self.

You have discovered a person incapable of being a truly reciprocal friend. Both the loss and the risk, however, are reduced to their appropriate size. It becomes your responsibility to verbalize your conclusion in a straightforward and unemotional statement: "You cannot accept me on my level, so I cannot accept you on yours." It is a clear and uncomplicated message, the result of your decision that further attempts at communication are not likely to succeed. The other person may come to understand, at some level, that what you have decided is the same conclusion he was willing to postpone or deny.

The process of sharing feelings involves being vulnerable, but the fact that you feel the other person cares is sufficient reason to take the risk. It is trust in the level of the listener's effectiveness, his willingness to share, that will, in turn, encourage you to disclose some of your self to him. If his attitude says, "I am here, ready and available, and willing to encourage you to look within yourself," you will take the challenge. As a result of looking deeper and reaching out, something new takes the place of the old. You have attained a higher level of self-awareness, expanding your ability to be in touch with your feelings and open yourself to another person. This is inner growth.

In addition, the fact that you chose that person as the listener is a tacit compliment. Any communication in the area of feelings and emotions promotes personal growth for both the speaker and the listener. Each of you grows through this new experience, as does the relationship.

Beware of Manipulation

When you become the listener in a dialogue, you may soon discover that the speaker is a person filled with insecurity, a dependent person who does not have an acceptance of himself which allows him to adequately contain and confront all his feelings. He is one who needs continuous reassurance and acceptance from others. His main motivation for entering such a conversation is to ask, rather than to share. He asks for advice, for love and acceptance, for your authoritarian approval, and for your value judgements. When you find yourself caught in such a negative situation, you must be aware that the speaker is not presenting himself honestly, that he is not willing to assume responsibility for who and what he is. On the contrary, he is asking that *you* assume this obligation for his inner life, that you take the responsibility for his feelings, his actions, and for their results.

As complimentary as it might feel to be looked up to as one capable of directing another's life, be wary of such a trap. You are being manipulated into assuming the tremendous responsibility for someone else's existence. It is an unreasonable request, because you cannot live his life. It is unwise to play the authority figure who hands down decisions. You cannot guide that person continuously— an unrealistic duty that he will immediately place upon you. You are actually inviting failure of the relationship because you will soon reach a point where you disappoint him. You will soon guide him incorrectly, and he will, of course, lay the blame on you without hesitation. In time, you will come to say, "I can't listen to you or advise you any longer." You will decide this out of a feeling of having been deceived. Your time and feelings have been wasted, and he is stripping you of your integrity, leaning on you.

Refuse to allow such a pattern to develop. When you realize someone is attempting this, your response should be, "I'm not ready or capable of making your decisions for you. I'm ready only to listen to you and to hear *your* decisions about what to do."

A relationship based on dependent need is not a lasting one. Two people drawn together because of such insecurity see the union as a source of outside strength. It is not going to work for long. They are robbing, leeching, leaning on each other—a relationship doomed to topple. If someone asks you a question such as, "What is your opinion?" or "What should I do?" be aware that you are being asked to take full responsibility for your answer. A *what* question can only be answered by the questioner, along with the assumption of responsibility for that answer. If not, the giver of advice is stepping into the trap. Only when you say, "I'd like to share my thoughts, and I'd like you to hear them without assuming responsibility for them," are you on the safe ground of two equals, two adequate adults.

Just as a child may ask, "Daddy, make a decision for me," there are times when an adult is in genuine need of direction. The contract in such a case must be clearly based on the fact that such a situation is immediate and temporary. The transaction must be unmistakable: "I need comfort from you right now." This must be countered by the clear understanding that the other person cannot be a source of comfort forever. No one is a self-sufficient adult at all times, but given such a request, you must be aware that the other is asking for an imbalance in the relationship. If a child's specific need requires that you enter the role of his "superego," as Freud terms it, also make it clear that he must grow to be his own adult. In a similar situation with a temporarily overwrought adult, make certain it is understood that the situation is temporary. In both cases, you must be sure the other person knows what he needs. He must understand that a temporary gift of help is quite different from assuming responsibility for his life.

Body Language

We cannot end this discussion of person-to-person communication without acknowledging the importance of *body language* in all human interactions. Until recently, the human body was relatively ignored as an important medium for increased understanding of the self, as well as for broadening our ability to communicate effectively with others.

In his book *Body Language*, Julius Fast reports that research by scientists indicates that over seventy percent of our communication with others is non-verbal. We transmit continuous messages through facial expressions and various other body movements, including such basic elements as the manner in which we talk, smile, sit, stand, and walk. Most of these messages are involuntary, and they are usually transmitted without our conscious knowledge. Most of the time we are quite unaware that we are clearly communicating our honest feelings of approval or disapproval, happiness or despair. These messages are particularly important and valid because of their unconscious spontaneity and their instinctive source. We cannot pretend, falsify, or manipulate them by means of conscious behavior. This area is therefore of great importance to those who wish to improve their communication of feelings. Learning to translate the symbols of body language is of immeasurable service to those who seek successful communication with self and with others.

Picturing the physical appearance and behavior of specific people will lead you to recall many of their unconscious body messages: the depressed or faltering walk with back slumped and head down; the erect and sturdy gait of the secure and positive individual; movement toward a person during conversation; direct eye contact by someone wishing to be close and involved; the moving back and looking away of a person who is uninterested, afraid, or in need of physical distance; the raising of eye-brows and its resultant widening of the eyes upon discovering a person or view that brings pleasure or surprise. We have all seen those people whose eyes sparkle with happiness and joy, just as we have seen the dissatisfied or disappointed man or woman with sagging face and drooping mouth—not to mention the obvious surrender of one who throws up his hands at the end of an argument, or the child who rushes to embrace a parent. The list is virtually endless.

Translating New Symbols of Body Language

Begin to watch deliberately for the body messages people around you are constantly sending. Many will fall in the category of the obvious, extreme, and familiar, such as the examples just given. Many others, however, are not so easily deciphered because you do not yet know their origin, or because you are not totally aware of the interplay of those involved. These can be discounted for the moment.

INCREASING AWARENESS OF BODY LANGUAGE

Look for recurring body messages. Once aware, you can often deduce what a given message means. Begin writing them down on a special list that you can add to daily. Become increasingly aware that similar messages are also emanating from your own body, and certainly include these. As a bonus, you will soon discover that certain movements of your own are highly personalized, but they nonetheless indicate specific responses. Pulling at your ear, for instance, might mean anything from annoyance and a wish to escape, to infatuation and interest. Some messages and mannerisms are primarily for the purpose of communication to self, an action meant for you alone to interpret. Because of this personalization in every individual, it is easy to misjudge. Add a ? after items on your list, unless you are absolutely certain.

Begin the list now, simply recalling some of the symbols of body language you have observed in the past. It will facilitate learning and increase the pace of this adventure if you adopt a personal kind of shorthand for your list. You might begin in this manner:

1. Slumped shoulders—defeat, depression
2. Eye contact—attention and interest
3. Frequent looking at watch—bored, anxious
4. Touching a body—emphasis, affection, desire
5. Raising of eyebrows—surprise, interest
6. Finger over mouth—hesitation (?)

The circumstances in which symbols occur often dictate their meaning. Depending on its cause, for example, a frown could mean anger, disgust, disapproval, concentration, fatigue, or merely excessive light hitting the eyes. You will also discover that body language is used in place of words, or directly preceding them. When startled, for instance, you react with your body before you verbalize, if you verbalize at all. You jump or tense *before* you say "Oh!" or scream. The order is never reversed unless it is a false and contrived response—such as the genuine open-eyed interest of a girl in response to a boy's attention *followed by* a calculated attempt at negation by the turning away of her head and saying, "I'm not interested." If research is correct, *seventy percent* of the time you will discover that you and others use the body in some fashion to express a feeling congruent with what you would have verbalized and, for a variety of reasons, did not.

Conduct this personal survey among the familiar people in your life. Of particular value are those at home or at work whom you see often and are of special interest. Your increased awareness of them will often suggest a pattern or profile—such as the employer who invariably frowns, the wife who is consistantly smiling, the child who is inordinately fearful and shy.

Check yourself as well, to see that the messages you give non-verbally are indeed honest indications of what you feel. Don't assume your appraisal is correct. Always check yourself for clarity and validity. Do the same with those close and intimate. "You just looked away and moved back when I approached you. Were you aware of that? Are you trying to tell me something?" Properly expressed, your verbal attempts to verify body language will seldom be rejected; such attempts are complimentary, practical, and expeditious. Continue by giving your interpretation of their message, whenever possible presenting the person with several choices: "I seem to pick up the message that you need some space and distance right now. It seems as if something is troubling you. Is it me? Am I coming on too strong; or am I interrupting something else on your mind? Would you prefer being left alone?"

Each time you attempt such a dialogue with someone, you are increasing your trust in the innate ability you are developing to read body language messages clearly and interpret them accurately. Secondly, in so doing you are verbalizing an interest and concern for the other person by implicitly communicating that how they feel matters to you. Finally, by clarifying your reactions, you will make significant people in your life increasingly aware that you have added a new and productive dimension to your relationship with them. By your example, they too may learn to grow sufficiently, and may well begin to react similarly toward you and toward others.

Comparing Body Messages to Verbal Messages

An amusing experience as well as an enlightening one is attending a cocktail party, or any similarly large gathering, and observing people's behavior as they all play the game called "Let's Pretend We Care." The rules are simple, perhaps explaining its wide-spread use. These participants have decided ahead of time that they are going to be very interested in everyone at the party, and not admit that in actual fact they don't give a damn. "Let's put on our charm and a nice big smile, and we'll show them how a smooth social operator works!" you can almost hear them promising themselves. With this preconditioning, body messages and verbal messages clash. Note how body messages reveal *true* feelings, while the speakers are busy attempting to cover them up with stereotyped and standard phrases. Stand apart and listen to the grand superlatives and false enthusiasm, and watch the empty bored faces that reveal the true feelings of the speaker. "How exciting for you!" a woman might say, looking around the room for the next person to approach. "How interesting!" a man will answer, fighting back the urge to yawn. Observe the hostess saying, "How very nice to meet you!" as she backs away, perhaps even looking away. "Fantastic!" you will hear, as the speaker looks again at his watch.

After your self-study, followed by observation of others, you will have begun mastering the basic symbols of body language. Knowledge of body language stimulates growth of communication between you and your inner self, and is also an essential element in honest and complete communication between you and others, especially those more important to you. Remember that most messages you send to friends, family, parents, and lovers are sent in non-verbal body language.

chapter 6

Finding Direction in Life

Meaning

A sense of self-esteem and positive self-assertiveness most easily rest upon the conviction that there is some meaning to one's life. Sooner or later, most of us get around to asking what the meaning of life is. If we go on asking this question, and cannot find answers, we begin to suffer what Paul Tillich has termed the anxiety of meaninglessness. For most of us, the only way to end this particular anxiety is either to abandon the question, accepting the fact that some questions simply cannot be answered within the sphere of human experience, or to make the leap of faith, and accept the explanation offered by a religion. It is not the purpose of this book to debate philosophy or theology; the question of religious belief must be dealt with in private, individual ways. We can, however, discuss the "meaning of meaning," and the general malady of "lack of meaning" in one's life.

First, consider the tremendous range of meanings attached to the word "meaning." It can be used to denote purpose, intent, significance, import, or design. Hence, when we ask, "What is the meaning of life?" or "What is the meaning of *my* life?" we generally seek an explanation

142

of the design and purpose of the world. Apart from faith, one cannot answer these questions with certainty. This has been an on-going quest for millenia—you will recall that Job asked what the meaning of life was, and knew he could not know. Even though this knowledge is denied us, and even knowing our life is limited, we *can* discover meaning in human activity and use the choices available to us in ways that give us a sense of purpose.

Before we go on, however, let me remind you that when many people complain of "meaninglessness" in their life, they are talking about something quite different from the philosophical frustrations mentioned above. Generally, the word is used as a substitute for another, more descriptive, term. For example, complaints such as "I have no sense of meaning in life" reduce to "I'm bored," or "I'm depressed," or "I haven't been able to commit myself to any clear goals." If you have been feeling that life is "meaningless," you will probably benefit greatly from trying to define more *specifically* what your disconcerting feelings are. If you discover that you actually are suffering from boredom, then having defined your problem, you are well on your way to coping with it!

Meaning and Personal Efficacy

In order to feel happy and fulfilled, everyone needs to feel he is of some significance and that his actions in this world matter. Everyone needs to be loved, to give love, and to feel important. These are the feelings that give us the *security* of relatedness—of interconnection with other people and the world as a whole. All of us doubt our significance, are bored, or have frustrations in our relationships at one time or another. Depression and boredom are part of the total self, and part of the cycle of life. Periodic bouts with them cannot be avoided. You cannot be happy all the time, but you *can* lend meaning to "low times" by viewing them as growth situations. There is great truth to the maxim that "a bad experience is truly bad only if you do not learn something from it." Even the most serious and disasterous situations still allow you to find something substantial in them. For example, let's say you go to the doctor and he tells you that you have terminal cancer and can expect to live only six months. Certainly, this is a situation you did not choose, and you may never really find a "purpose" in your death. Living for years and years is not a choice available to you, but you can exercise the choices which are available to you! You can decide how to spend your last months—you can resolve to make them wonderful months with your loved ones, instead of wasting them by bewailing your fate. The meaning of any situation is: What positive value we can extract from it?

In situations like the example given above, people respond by finding meaning in two basic ways. Some people—generally those with great religious faith—can find meaning by seeing themselves as an instrument of a greater force, being used or fulfilling a mission in the name of a grand design. Others find meaning through the definition of their own purposes and the choice among options available to them. In this way, they can "control" at least a limited sphere of their environment, and view such control as an important, meaningful mode of self-expression.

The Need for Value Definition

Depending upon our religious convictions, we may or may not feel we understand the "ultimate meaning of life." However, even people who describe themselves as "basically religious" suffer from a generalized discontent which they describe as a "lack of a sense of meaning" in *daily life*. This is a widely noted phenomenon, and is related to the decline of those institutions which, in past centuries, dictated the values and meanings of life's activities—i.e., rigid social systems, powerful churches, absolute monarchs, etc.

As Western man has come to be less and less responsible to authoritarian values, he finds himself in the position of needing to develop his own humanistic values. Insofar as humanistic values are individually defined, this task is extremely difficult; many people fear they are not capable of bearing the responsibility for defining their own values, and so they resort to conformism—patterning their values after those of others, whether these be parents, admired friends, or famous people. This can be destructive to the individual. Mindless adoption of someone else's values deprives a person of the growth-producing experience of introspecting and discovering his own value structure. And, to the extent that he is unaware of his real values, an individual is divorced from knowing himself.

The search for a sense of meaning in daily life best begins with a consideration of individual values. The core of a meaning-oriented life can be the resolve, "I want to do the best I can to live out my sense of values." An awareness of your values, and an awareness of how each of your actions fits in to your value framework, gives you a sense of relatedness to a whole. Therefore, one must work on the discovery and clarification of his values.

Value Hierarchy

Once you have become familiar with your values, you can proceed to an exploration of the hierarchy of these values. That is to say, you must discover the priority of each value. This is an exercise that is usually new to most people, who tend to assume all "values" exist on the same plane. In reality, values are seldom of equal weight; they differ by degree of importance to our inner sense of self.

An awareness of this, and of the hierarchy of your set of values, is extremely valuable. In times of inner turmoil, if it becomes evident that two or more values are involved and seemingly in conflict, a knowledge of value priorities allows you to quickly resolve the conflict, and save yourself from much anguish.

In dealing with value hierarchies, there is a common pitfall to avoid. Many people mistakenly feel that favoring one value over another is tantamount to a rejection of the other. This is not true. You are as deeply committed to the other value as before; you have simply acknowledged hierarchy. An obvious example of this might be provided by the case of the woman who cherished two values (among others): to be kind and considerate of her friends, and to be a good mother. If an "emergency" were to arise with one of her children, she might have to be rude—for example, not show up for a luncheon appointment with her friend. No one would question her action, for we all understand that some things are "more compelling" than others.

In summary, then, the first step you can take towards building a sense of meaning into your life is to work out a clear awareness of your sense of values. This enables you to make choices with these in mind, and thereby imparts to your actions a sense of connectedness to a meaningful whole. Your actions are significant, in that they reflect the living-out of your sense of values. In this regard, you must develop your ability to recognize, or be aware of, the way in which your choices fit into your value framework. Most choices you have to make relate to your values, and by being aware of the relationships, even mundane actions take on a greater sense of importance.

A word of caution: you need not feel your set of values must include dedication to great social works, altruistic sacrifices, and so on. Your values may find their best manifestation in your relationships with family and friends, in job performance, or in some other facet of daily life. In the long run, living by making choices which are congruent, insofar as possible, with your value hierarchy will enhance your sense of personal satisfaction, enjoyment, and pleasure in life. In this way, we can truly say that the pursuit of values brings happiness. However, this is not to say that everything you do in the fulfillment of your values will necessarily be pleasurable in the doing. As an example, let us suppose that you have defined human kindness and compassion as being one of your paramount values. You have an elderly woman neighbor, and you discover that she is dying of terminal illness. You know she has no kin, and no money, and therefore will be put into a county home with minimal custodial care when she becomes too ill to care for herself. You have a choice: you can avoid involvement, involve yourself partially (helping, and visiting for example), or involve yourself totally (committing yourself to care for her). If you decide you wish to take on the burden of her care yourself, because this is the decision most congruent with your value framework, it will not be a joyous task. It will probably be depressing and sad and unpleasant in many ways. But, because you acted with an awareness of the meaning of the act in mind, you will later derive much satisfaction from the knowledge that you did a compassionate deed which was an act of commitment to your dearest values. (Note: a person who chose not to care for the elderly neighbor would not necessarily display himself as being unkind. He might have other commitments or values which take precedence.)

Meaning and Goals

A sense of meaning can also be the by-product of self-fulfilling activity. As we have described in earlier chapters, the self-fulfilling person is one who identifies his dreams and mobilizes his talents to achieve his dreams. A person who is living in this mode feels his actions, the days of his life, have meaning because they are *goal-directed*, and further, aimed at goals he has set in the depths of his being. It is obvious that the choice of your goals, and of plans to achieve them, involve guidance by your values and furnish a rough definition of you as a person. You must recognize the significance in this, and incorporate it into your self-concept. We might add that activities you do *not* choose to pursue also serve as self-definition: you might well say to yourself, "I don't want to do that, because it goes against my personal ethics."

When it comes to goal-setting, many people are bewildered by a notion that they must have grand, sweeping life goals which fit into the sentence, "In my life, I have it as my goal to . . ." This frightens most people, and breeds a sense of inadequacy ("I really don't know what I want to do with my life over the long run"). My advice is that if the concept of "life goals" bothers you at all, forget them! Think instead in terms of long-range goals (what you want to accomplish in the next three years), short-range goals (to be achieved in the next year), and very short-range goals (things which you want to see happen now).

Goal Definition

Goal-directed activity must begin with a clear notion of what you wish to achieve; in order to be effective and satisfying, it must focus on selected goals, reflecting a clear sense of personal priorities.

CLARIFYING GOALS AND PRIORITIES

In order to achieve a forthright sense of purpose, you can begin by making a list of what is important to you in life. These may be things you wish to experience (love, parenthood, creative ecstasy) and/or things you want to achieve (a college degree, a higher salary, good grades in school). In other words, you will find that you have some goals related to achievement, and others relating to your relationships with others.

Now, go through the list and mark each goal either "necessary" or "negotiable." In other words: which are absolutely necessary to your personal fulfillment and happiness, and which are negotiable (much desired, but less critical to your happiness). This gives you a look at your priorities. No cheating! You cannot mark every goal as "necessary." No one needs—or gets—all his goals. By making the difficult selection of necessary vs. negotiable goals you are making the first step towards the fulfillment of your dreams—because you will now be able (if need be) to sacrifice the negotiables in order to get the necessaries. This means you have more flexibility in pursuit of the things which you *really need*.

After you have made this preliminary division of priorities, try to sense the intensity of your feelings connected with each goal. Go through the list of "necessary" goals, and, about each one, ask yourself "How much do I really want this?" You will probably find that your *will* is much greater to accomplish some goals than others. Will is the commitment to act; you may intellectually want something very much, you may emotionally desire it very much, but you may have very little will to see it through—to "make it happen." Pick the goal which has the strongest "will component" already attached to it and begin by focusing on it. As you work to realize it, you will feel purposeful, and eventually (if not initially) energized.

Difficulties in Goal Definition

I have sometimes encountered people who tell me that they "want to want something," but that they just don't want anything! This is a trap, and is useless suffering in response to the feeling that one *should* "want things" (i.e., have specific goal orientations). There is no reality to a "want to want." If you don't want anything—at the moment—this is what you want; you want to be left alone. Sometimes we need periods (even long periods of time) to waste, to live in the here and now, with no internal or external pressures to do or to want things. This is very meaningful as a phase of self-development (and perhaps expanded self-awareness). You could just say that it is meaningful to you to have a life without pressure.

Another problem encountered in the clarification of goals comes when one expects to have constant goals. Your goals—what is meaningful and satisfying to you— may change daily or periodically. You are not static, so your meaning-orientations won't be static either. The more general your definitions of your goals, the more— seemingly!—"constant" your goals are. For example: if I say it is meaningful for me to be a good mother to my children by staying at home with them, and then a few months later I decide that I must go back to work to save my sanity, have my goals changed? If you examine the mundane level, yes they have. Before, my goal was to stay at home and now it is to get out of the home. However, on a more general plane, my goal seems constant: to be a good mother to my children and to obtain self-satisfaction. It is only my strategy, or plan, as to how to obtain these goals that has altered. I have discovered I am so dissatisfied staying at home, I can't be a good mother or fulfilled person; so I decided that I would be a better mother if I fulfilled my own needs too, and got out of the house regularly.

Another pitfall people encounter when they try to define the "meanings" in their life is their own fear of (external) value judgments. We are so thoroughly socialized to be other-oriented that we try to find goals which are meaningful to us *and* acceptable to others. We want our goals to be respectable, laudable, "worthy." Let's assume that you know in the depths of your heart that your *real* goal for the summer months is to get a suntan and lose weight. This is fine. Don't torture yourself about it. Just do it, and get the satisfaction from accomplishing it! The danger lies in a self-critical approach which says, "That isn't much of a goal. If I had any substance to me, I'd have some important goal, like doing volunteer work or going to college summer session or something like that." This kind of self-berating is destructive, and serves no useful purpose; you will not reform yourself, you will only make yourself unhappy. Stop and realize that your self-torture is based on the assumption that some goals are "more meaningful" than others. *Given a sufficiently skeptical outlook, you can deny meaning in almost every activity in life*–and who is there to decisively refute you? You can question the "worth" of parenting, of business, of doctoring, of teaching, of gardening, of homemaking—the list is endless. And you will be right! There is no worth in any activity except as experienced by the human beings acting or affected. You discover what is meaningful to you, and experience the meaning which comes from acting purposefully.

Recapitulation

In order to achieve a meaning-orientation in your activities and goals, there are two steps, with several substeps:

Step 1: Set your priorities. Do this by clarifying your goals. Don't put down your goals, respect them. Realize that these are your current goals—that they may change—but these are what you are dealing with now.

Step 2: Plan to achieve your goals. This must be a *practical* plan with step-by-step (practical) stages/actions for achieving your goals. Muster your energy and assertiveness to the commitment to this plan. Make a contract with yourself to carry out this plan.

In working through these steps, you must undertake the following activities:

(1) List your priorities for what you want to achieve/

experience in 3 months, 6 months, 1 year, 5 years.
Don't feel you are being asked to predict or foreswear
the future—your goals and priorities, of course, may
change, but looking ahead from the perspective of
how you feel at this moment helps you to evaluate
your goals (i.e., discern which are necessary and
which are negotiable) and helps suggest action-plans
for achieving them.

(2) Assess the obstacles to achievement of your goals,
then plan to overcome—or avoid—the obstacles.

(3) Write down specific stages of action to be undertaken
in order to achieve your goals (necessary goals).

(4) Make a list of alternates and substitutes which can—if
need be—be used to replace *specific* goals in order to
achieve *general* goals. Be prepared to accept these alternates where first-designated goals are unattainable.
In this way, you will not become locked in long
periods of frustration and meaning-vacuums; you
have flexibility, and because you know that you have
this, you have a more positive attitude (and greater
courage—strength, if you prefer the word) with which
to pursue your goals.

Substitute Goals

Apparently, the concept of having substitute, or alternate
goals is a very difficult one for many idealistic people to
accept. There is widespread belief that the surest way to
attain those things you really want is to refuse compromise! I reject this kind of thinking. Compromise is an
extremely important element in achieving life's satis-
factions—it gives us flexibility and adaptability, which are
keys to happiness. When you discover that the achievement of one goal is foreclosed to you, then you must act to
achieve the alternative to that particular goal. Don't proceed by thinking, "I can't have what I want, so I'll have to

accept the compromise." Instead, *shift* your goal-focus, making the compromise your goal, and abandoning your original goal.

You might ask how one easily shifts his goal from X to Y. This is most easily done if Y was defined at the same time that X was established as a goal. Once you have wedded yourself to a specific outcome (X), and then that doesn't happen, it is, of course, difficult to change your focus (to Y). Thus, the critical importance of defining alternatives and compromises from the very outset of establishing your priorities.

A friend of mine provides a concrete illustration. She married late, and was determined to have a baby of her own. Her husband was agreeable, and so they proceeded with plans for a child. However, months passed into years, and no baby came. My friend was increasingly depressed, locked into frustration of her goal. One day, in anguish, she asked me, "How can I quit wanting what I want?" Certainly, she can "be mature" and do her best to "accept" her disappointment, but it was extremely difficult for her to simply quit wanting her own baby. How much easier it would have been for her if she had adopted a more flexible goal-orientation at the outset! For example, she might have said to herself, "I would really like to have my own baby, and that is my first choice; however, if I can't have a baby of my own, then I prefer to continue working and use all that extra money we'll have to take a fabulous trip every summer." Or, "I would like to have my own child, but if that doesn't work out, then we'll apply for adoption." Either of these orientations would leave her with positive actions, well-defined in advance, which can be used to further the ultimate goal of self-fulfillment. Neither are deserving of that common accusation, "negative thinking."

Abusive Approaches to Personal Growth

est—An Abusive Approach to Humanistic Psychology

When Werner Erhard decided to create his own super-organization for cashing in on the mind-expanding personal-improvement market, I'm sure he was carefully, personally aware of the neat coincidence between the name of his movement—est—and its central maxim. The name, in Latin, means "it is," and in Erhard's philosophy, this is Truth ("What is, is. What isn't, isn't.").

Erhard has grossed millions selling this message to thousands of "trainees," who have paid hefty fees to experience "Truth." Considering the fact that the est organization was founded only in 1971, this is no small accomplishment. But then, Werner Erhard has a long past history of salesmanship—including apprenticeships with selling correspondence courses, encyclopedias, and mind dynamics. The number of people who have been converted to est-think is sobering. My concern is that est training is based on practices and techniques which are the antithesis of humanism, individualism, and freedom. For this reason, I have singled out est for discussion as an abusive approach to humanistic psychology.

Est runs seminars, "training seminars," in major cities from coast-to-coast, with a tuition ($250 in 1975 when I

154

attended a seminar) for a full two-weekend (approximately 70 hours) experience. Two or three hundred people are simultaneously trained, and so this process is one which takes on ballroom-size proportions. After "graduation," trainees are invited to continue participation in "graduate seminars," which provide a continued infusion of the est message, and which insure a continuous link to the est organization. The graduate seminars are relatively low-cost in tuition, and est claims that they are actually "money-losers," but even as such, they are pretty cheap from an organizational standpoint, since they provide est with its lifeblood—new recruits. From the outset, est has eschewed commercial advertising, and has relied upon word-of-mouth recruitment of "trainees" for its major seminars. It has also operated with a small paid staff, and used an army of volunteers to do office work and help run training sessions. This army of faithful workers and proselytizers is maintained through the use of graduate seminars to keep people linked to the organization.

What does est offer? Erhard himself has officially stated that, "The purpose of the est training is to transform your ability to experience living so that the situations you have been trying to change, or have been putting up with, clear up just in the process of life itself." At least, this is what a major est brochure claims. The potential est trainee never comes any closer to a specific statement of what est is all about, because, as est-people so smugly put it, "You have to experience it, you can't describe it." Even graduates are enjoined from describing their est experience to other people. To be sure, they are urged to bring others to est "Guest Programs"—where they are pressured to sign up for training themselves, but they are cautioned not to describe the est "process" for fear that this would "ruin it " for their friends.

With such a vague, yet somehow glittering, come-on, what is the appeal of est? It promises to fix your life. "If

your life isn't working, maybe it's time to look elsewhere."
This is an extremely powerful appeal, especially in an era
when every social discipline documents the crumbling of
the social fabric and the desolate sense of anomie experienced by modern man. It is the *commonplace* perception,
that life "isn't working," so think of the marketplace
touched by this little est theme! This appeal is especially
potent because of the general acceptability gained by ex-
perimentation in "far out" movements over the last dec-
ade. It has become downright chic in some circles to talk of
Gestalt, Transcendental Meditation, Rolfing, Scientology,
Arica, Tai Chi-chuan, and so on. Hence, the ease with
which one can move on to yet another experiment. If past
experiences haven't "worked," then try this new approach. Ironically, this appeal runs counter to the ultimate
message of est, which is that only *you* can make things
work. So you buy an experience, believing that it will "fix
you up." Perhaps it is just this belief in *methods* that sets
the stage for the experience which ultimately follows—the
uncritical acceptance of the methods practiced by est because these are people "who know," and are therefore
your natural superiors.

There is another strong appeal in the est come-on: est
apparently *does* work for many people, or at least it seems
irrefutable that there are hundreds of shining-eyed est
graduates testifying that "est changed my life." Given this
fact, the tuition fee seems a real bargain.

Est also exudes respectability. Witness its sheer size.
People respect success and power, and tend to accept
manifestations of success as signs of worthiness. Any organization that has grown as dramatically as est must have
something good to offer. Also witness the respectable professional people who go to est. Est repeatedly emphasizes
the number of its trainees who are educators, profession-
als, or executives—no rag-tag outfit, this! If you go to a
training seminar, you most assuredly will find yourself in

the midst of people you can relate to. And you might be comforted to know that est has a prestigious advisory board, whose president is the ex-chancellor of the University of California Medical Center. Obviously, if you are contemplating spending a few hundred dollars for training, you are soothed to know that these aren't just quacks or hippies who endorse the program. In fact, the federal government has given est a contract to run its training program in selected school districts. So, est appears "safe."

Best of all, word has seeped out that est training ultimately convinces you that *you are OK*. Everyone wants to feel that he is "OK"—especially those people who are considering est, or else why would they be seeking such a program to "make life work"? What a relief to feel, to be convinced, that you don't have to be other than what you are. You don't have to become anything. In this sense, perhaps est is appealing to an anxiety that has been set up by the growth and human potential movement, the anxiety that you must become something other than what you are.

At any rate, the appeal of est is easily seen. A cheap and respectable way of fixing your life and making you love yourself. It is also—although this is not quite so apparent until later—a means of allowing you to "fit" in society. Est tells you that you are perfect as you are, and introduces you to a body of thinking (a quasi-ideology) which supports this conclusion, and to an organization which supports your endorsement of this ideology. Therefore, you fit, you are OK, you are a part of something. This offers a wonderful sense of belonging and acceptance, periodically reaffirmed by "graduate seminars." As the numbers of est graduates grow, each graduate will increasingly feel that he not only fits into something, but that he fits into a social movement of important proportions. Where will this lead? Perhaps only Werner Erhard can tell us.

As a counselor and educator, I was interested in est as a phenomenon, and as a potentially useful new tool in the personal growth movement, so I signed up to attend the two-weekend training program. Despite the barrage of literature I received prior to the date of the training, I was still taken aback by the organizational efficiency—the almost overwhelming army of training assistants—who greeted our band of two hundred and fifty trainees on the first morning. I use the word "army" purposely, for it seemed that virtually all of the leaders and helpers were dressed alike in expensive clothes and shining shoes with carefully styled "mod" haircuts and fixed smiles. All this seemed to convey the message that this was an organization of those who had "made it," and that you, too, could join them and partake of the good life. I noted that their clothing was generally brown or black—a fact which, upon later consideration, reminded me of a military movement, using uniform and unity as a means of asserting authority and superiority.

We were issued name tags and ushered into a large room, where hundreds of hard chairs were carefully arranged in groups. At first, there was a general buzz of conversation among the trainees, until a leader appeared and abruptly warned us that there was to be no talking. Then, to a hushed—chastised—audience, the leader barked out the "ground rules" which were to prevail throughout the training experience. We were to remain in our hard seats at all times, speaking only if recognized. Leaving the room at any time other than at official breaks was expressly prohibited (there would be, we were told, a maximum of two breaks per day). This meant that we were to go for stretches of six to eight hours without being allowed to go to the bathroom or move about. Smoking and eating were also prohibited. Of course, we were not to tell others about the "est method" or what we were experiencing.

These "rules" set the authoritarian tone for all that was to follow. And yet, from the very outset, we were told that we were free individuals, in that we were "agreeing" to abide by these rules; anyone who didn't agree was warned to leave immediately. So there you had it: stay and be bossed (but free), or leave and enjoy your freedom in ignorance. Most people remained. A sense of excitement filled the air, for this was a new experience for all who had never been in a concentration camp. As a result, a self-selected audience remained; we had made the commitment to "play ball."

Once the rules were accepted, they were strictly enforced. If one dared to whisper to a neighbor, an est "helper" rushed forward to hush you up; if one slouched in his chair, he was abruptly told to sit up straight. Most distressing to me, we were not allowed to take notes or write anything down! We were to "experience," not observe. This control over the environment in which we existed was a critical element in all that was to follow. As the leader put it, "We're going to tear you down and put you back together." Then, he proceeded to do so.

In the process of tearing us down, the leader of the "seminar" told us that we were all "assholes," and from that point forth, assholes we were called. We *deserved* to be called this, it seemed, because we were stupid enough to think that someone or something else had made our lives a mess, whereas in reality we ourselves were responsible for the disarray of our lives. We were assholes for trying to understand life at all, because, "In life, understanding is the booby prize." Every belief, reason, understanding or logic was labelled "non-experience," and therefore worthless. In fact, we were told, man can't really reason at all, but simply responds to stimuli (situations) by churning out reasons and "positions" to justify and defend himself. So forget it. Belief systems don't work; you can't reason;

you shouldn't try to understand life. Don't even try to respond to this experience by trying to figure it out or by questioning it: "It's done because Werner found that it works."

Imagine the confusion this creates. But even confusion, we are told, is part of the process: "Confusion is the first step towards 'natural knowing.'" So it all ties up into a neat little package: trust none of your reason, reject your cherished beliefs, disregard your confusions, and *have faith* in est! Mark Brewer, a freelance journalist in the San Francisco Bay Area, has analyzed this process so well that I draw upon his words to summarize the effects of such an environment upon the individuals present:

> Such efforts, of course, are commonly known as *brainwashing*, which is precisely what the est experience is, and the result is usually a classic conversion. . . . By distorting the fundamental stimulus-response mechanisms of eating, moving, sleeping, smoking a cigarette or going to the john, while [the leader] bombarded them hour after hour about how their lives and their thinking were all fucked up, the training would shake, confuse and finally, in a great majority of cases, dislodge the old ideas and behavior patterns. And then in would go the desired est perceptions, and ultimately the notion that you are perfect the way you are.*

Once the trainees are softened up for the message, it is delivered: You are responsible for your life situation. No one else can be blamed; no excuses are allowed. All of your complaining is really to be laid at your own two feet. It is an est "premise" that everyone has a "position" to defend, and that this position leads to almost mechanical, repetitive patterns of behavior. The est leader tries to "smoke out" and expose each person's "position," and in so doing, make each person aware of how automatically

---

*Mark Brewer, "We're Gonna Tear You Down and Put You Back Together," *Psychology Today*, August 1975, p. 39.

he repeats the patterns of behavior that comprise his present unhappy life. For example, one woman complained that she was an alcoholic because her husband was cruel and unloving. The leader immediately shouted, "BULLSHIT!" The lady was an alcoholic, he said, because she had chosen to respond to her husband in that way. She, and she alone, was responsible for her life scene. On and on it went, as each trainee who ventured forth an objection or an exception to "the rule," was thunderously rebuked for offering *excuses* for his life.

Once this process was complete, depression lay heavy throughout the hall. We were assholes, miserable assholes, and it was our own fault. None of our beliefs could help us, and we were unable to reason. It seemed that the message could get no worse, but it did. Finally, we were told, we are machines, and can't be anything other than what we are. For this discovery we paid $250!

"You're a machine." Your mind has no choice about the stimuli it receives or the responses it initiates. Therefore, you can't be anything other than what you are—an asshole-machine. Since most of us felt we had miserable lives, this message seemed like a death sentence: You are responsible for your misery, but you should accept it, because you are a machine and your life couldn't have been other than what it is. Yech. Locked into a worthless, unsatisfying life.

Just at this point, when gloom was so thick you could cut it with a knife, the leader offered us "Salvation." Your life is the way it is because of the stimulus-response patterns in your mind. But you freely chose this life of yours, because *you* created your mind, you created the stimulus-response patterns that comprise your mind. You, you see, are quite powerful after all! You're perfect, in that you created perfect truth (what is), and you have perfect power (to choose what will be). All you have to do is accept this, and you've "got it." Recognize that you are responsible for your responses to things, and that by choosing your responses to people and situations, you create what you get in life. As you continue living, you will choose the future. Don't *try* to change. Just relax, and as you go on living, change will occur. Got it?

At this point, about 80 percent of the trainees "got it." Shuffles, sighs, moans of pleasure filled the room. The leader invited those who "got it" to share their enlightenment with the others, and eager helpers ran forward with microphones as person after person attested to the new vision of life he had gained. The pressures to join the bandwagon and proclaim that you, too, had "gotten it" became immense. And the *intimidation* became intense.

I, for one, had courage to proclaim that I had not "gotten it." I stood to criticize the est message, but was immediately cut off and told that my remarks were "not appropriate." It seems that only "sharing" (read "agreeing") remarks are invited. We were repeatedly told to stand up if we had not yet "gotten it." Each time, there were fewer who stood. Of course, this was a means of singling out the hold-outs and making us feel humiliated and conspicuous. No further elaboration of "it" was offered, we were simply told to think about it until we "got it." I suspect that most people buckled under to the pressures for conformity and their own need for inclusion (or perhaps their sheer exhaustion and the need to go home), for finally, when the leader called for all who had not yet "gotten it" to stand up, I stood alone. I was congratulated by others afterwards for "having courage," and it chills me to think that this process was such that it would require unthinkable (for so many, it seems) courage to say, "I don't understand, and I'm not going to pretend that I do."

Why is est an *abusive* approach to personal growth?

To be sure, there are many general truths to be found in the *message* conveyed by est—truths with which it would be difficult to find fault. For example, what professional in psychological counseling would not agree that it is important for each individual to take responsibility for his own life, to acknowledge "authorship" of his present life situation and to accept the task of choosing his own future? But just because general truths comprise a portion of est's teaching, does not exempt the organization, or the method, from critical scrutiny.

The *method* employed by est is probably the most objectionable to me, for the methods are inimical to true personal growth. I am unwilling to endorse est simply "because it works." I am not convinced that it "works," but there certainly are thousands of est graduates willing to give enthusiastic testimonials. With great sincerity, they avow that, as a result of their est training, they are happier, have a new sense of release, or somehow are more in control of their own life. Obviously, est has done something for them. But *what* has it done? Has it led them to *personal growth*? Or has est used indoctrination and pressure tactics (read *brainwashing*) to sell a package of ideas which simply define the individual as happy? I suspect that the latter is the case.

Personal *growth* comes through the experience of one's inner feelings and the acceptance and understanding of one's true self. I, for one, could not achieve this in the environment created by est. I do not feel free to focus inwardly and experience my true feelings in an atmosphere of supersalesmanship, regimentation, and constant abuse. This is an atmosphere of intimidation, one in which "helpers" race down the aisles to tell me that I am not sitting up straight in my chair, that I cannot take notes, that I may not eat my piece of candy. Am I an adult, or am I a child? Am I free, or a prisoner? One quickly becomes confused. I am continuously called four-letter words, so that I will experience "greater aliveness." Am I more alive as an "asshole," than as a woman? Growth comes in conjunction with personal affirmation—I grow as I learn to respect myself, or as I service my self-respect; but I cannot find the portion of myself which I *respect* (which is the basis for self-esteem) when I am driven only towards those portions of myself which are to be held in *contempt*. If the "leaders" have such contempt for me, must I not conclude that I am deserving of contempt—even self-contempt?

Growth involves the acceptance of the self as unique. I cannot differentiate myself, and express my uniqueness, in a group where I am made to feel like an outcast, a moron, an "asshole" for admitting that I haven't "gotten the message."

Growth is of necessity an individual process, involving self-determination. It does not come from taking steps with the purpose of gaining group acceptance. And yet this is the process in est sessions. When people claim that they "get it," they are applauded and hugged. When they question or criticise, they are cut off, with clear indications that they are too inferior to question superior knowledge.

Growth comes when the sense of responsibility for one's life is centered in the self. Yet, est claims that the human mind is nothing but a stimulus-response machine—and this is exactly how est treats human trainees. The ultimate "getting it" is based on appeals to accept a message/method "because Werner knows it works." This *acceptance of authority* is indeed a machine-like mentality. The end achieved through automatism, not human conviction. You are told that "you are OK" But to really feel OK, you must have confidence in yourself and your values. Growth is based on a clarification of the individual value system, and a squaring of your own choices with your own system of values. But est sees all value systems (belief systems) other than its own as being "nonsense." This severely limits your options for growth, and certainly removes the possibility of a spiritual dimension in human development.

So far, I have focused on my objections to est as a

movement in the area of personal growth. I also have severe reservations concerning the implications of est as a movement in a democratic society. Any movement which encourages acceptance of authority without questioning, demands suspension of mental faculties, and disrespects the individual nature of personal growth, is encouraging exactly those characteristics which form the basis for an autocratic movement. We must be very careful when we see a situation in which an organization like est receives federal funding to train school children in this fashion, for this is a sign that our educational institutions are not discriminating between humanistic values and demagogic practices. Humanistic education, like democracy, must be based on a philosophy which respects the individuality and rationality of each person, the freedom to choose among belief systems, the necessity of questioning and understanding as the basis for self-responsibility. If we abandon these ideals, in the name of "getting it," we may *get* other than personal freedom.

Some Final Words . . .

It is hard to change your entire outlook about selfishness. We all experience this difficulty, because from childhood onward we are taught that being selfish is "bad." But you need to change your concept of selfishness, and you need also to change your way of life in order to accommodate it. Every day, say to yourself, "What can I do for myself? I like myself; I am responsible for this day being a special day, and for my life being a fulfilling life."

I know that this often seems hard to put into practice, so perhaps it will help if you remind yourself that it *is* a matter of choice. You can live up to the demands of others, or you can live out your own needs and potentialities. You can choose to be the nice person that "everyone likes," even at the price of your own happiness! Many people do try to be universally liked, and end up constantly serving others—and resenting it. How many times do *you* resent "having to do" those "nice things" you do, simply because you cannot bring yourself to say no to a request? There are people whose lives are literally swamped by little services to friends and acquaintances—writing letters for others, taking neighbors to the store, listening to boring complaints, and so on. We all do some of these things, of course. And hopefully, we do them because we *want* to. The problem arises when you find yourself doing more and more of these services because you are *afraid* that if you say no, you are a "bad," selfish person. If you lead your life in this way, you may in fact someday receive a gold medal (but don't count on it). Or, your tombstone could be inscribed, "He did everything for others." But what will you have done for yourself?

The other choice is to accept the fact that some people will love you and others will not like you at all—and so what? If you can live with such a "mixed judgment," you will progressively care less and less about the judgments of other people. If you accept the concept of positive selfishness, you are really saying, "I accept the fact that some people will not like me, but I am convinced that this is the way *I* want to live my life, and I am happy." This attitude resolves your inner conflict, and removes your overwhelming need to look outside yourself for positive reinforcement, for someone else to tell you that you're OK. You must convince yourself that you love yourself, and once you're convinced, you're on the road to a more self-respecting and fulfilling life. The most difficult task lies at the outset: to *reeducate* yourself by learning that you *deserve* to be positively selfish.

In this book, we have attempted to guide you towards a new life orientation. A happier life is not something that happens automatically. We cannot say that after doing 20 or 30 exercises you will have "arrived." Anyone who would claim such a thing is offering a gimmick—and a sham. However, we have offered an approach which you can use to start your new way of life. As your life unfolds, a multitude of situations present themselves, little things that we have not included in this book. Whether these things appear to you to be trivial or crucial, you must say to yourself, "Wait! What is this to me? I like myself enough to first of all care for my needs and my decisions. Strong, impressive, manipulating people are not going to make my decisions for me, because *I'm* responsible for what happens in my life. I will act in a way that makes me feel comfortable. I will not allow myself to be indoctrinated or intimidated."

In order to work towards the resolution of personal problems and the attainment of positive selfishness, you must have an ongoing dialogue with yourself. In conventional therapy you would have a dialogue with your therapist; instead, develop the habit of writing in a journal. That will make you a better counselor for yourself. We have attempted to introduce you to a framework for approaching and resolving personal difficulties. Learning to use this approach—and working through it honestly and patiently—requires time, and some personal suffering, on your part. But the rewards will be well worth the investment. I mention suffering because there is always a certain amount of pain involved when you plow through your inner being and attempt to change. Give yourself sympathy when you encounter this pain—but don't let the pain stop your work towards self-revelation and problem-resolution.

Whenever you tackle a problem, begin by a careful assessment of *your definition* of the situation. Often, you will find that you have foreclosed options for dealing with the problem by the way in which you define it. At times, you will discover that the use of certain adjectives in describing the problem adds an unnecessary element of dread or failure to your perception of reality. If you find that particular descriptive *words* evoke definite negative responses in you, then work to define and describe your problem using totally different vocabulary. This will help you objectify the problem, and make it easier for you to approach its resolution in creative ways.

After you have reassessed the problem and its definition, take an *inventory* of the ways in which it affects you. This inventory should always be written in your journal, for it will be a valuable tool for future reference.

The next step is a rational exercise: Construct a *plan of action* for working to overcome the problem. The most important aspect of this plan is that it must provide *incremental* steps, or phases. Since few of us are able to change well-established patterns of behavior easily in one fell swoop, the likelihood of success in changing is boosted if we recognize that change *is* difficult, and undertake it on a gradual basis.

Once the plan is made, you must *carry it out*. This is the point of true commitment—action. If you have built an incremental plan, the first step should not be too difficult to face. Just remember, you can do it, if you want to!

When you have implemented the first step of your plan, do not feel you then have to rush on to the next step. Establish each new behavior carefully before adding to it. Repeat and repeat the activity. This serves as good practice, and also has other important effects.

Every time you act in your own benefit, and really feel comfortable about the things you do, your process of change is reinforced. This is what we call positive reinforcement, for it builds your willingness to take further risks, and risks are always a part of personal change. You risk self-assertion and discover, "Ah, I asserted myself and other people still accept me. The world is not my enemy. It's too bad if some don't agree with me, but then I'm not living for other people. I'm convinced that my position is the best for me." This *feels good*, and therefore reinforces your self-esteem. These are the building blocks that create a whole new way of life.

Positive selfishness will always require effort. All of us have weaknesses and vulnerabilities which can crop up. For example, you might feel that you need your mother to be proud of you, and that you consequently will do whatever she expects of you. Or, you might need your spouse to think that you're the greatest in all respects, and therefore dare not disappoint his/her expectations of you. Some people need the approval of their teenage children, and try to act "hip" in order to obtain it. But in such cases, weigh carefully both consequences of your action: you may do things which *please others*, and cause them to adore you, but the person adored *will not be the real you*. It will be the you that is acting in order to be accepted, in order to receive strokes. Is this the price you want to pay for adoration?

At such times, when you are tempted to let the demands or expectations of others manipulate you, or when you lose the inner confidence that a constructive selfishness is the best route to happiness, you need concrete reminders of the rewards of positive selfishness. You can supply these reminders for yourself with the personal journal you keep as you go through the process of change. Write down in this journal your anxieties, your actions, and your accomplishments. Then, when you feel vulnerable, re-read your journal and you will find strong support for your conviction that you must serve yourself before you serve others. You will not please everyone, but you will create for yourself a full, rich, rewarding life.

BOOKS OF RELATED INTEREST

In SELF-ESTEEM / A DECLARATION, world-renowned family therapist Virginia Satir presents an essential credo for the individual in modern society. 64 pages, soft cover, $2.95

In MAKING CONTACT, Virginia Satir draws on years of experience and observation, and a rich understanding of human potential and interaction, to show how you can better understand and use the basic tools for making contact with others. She clearly explains reliable techniques that will make it possible for you to work for change in your perceptions, your actions, and your life. 96 pages, soft cover, $3.95

SELECTIVE AWARENESS by Dr. Peter H.C. Mutke demonstrates the power of selective awareness in reprogramming negative thought/ emotion patterns to promote physical health, healing, and the undoing of destructive habits such as overeating, smoking, insomnia, and pain. 240 pages, soft cover, $4.95

In SELF-CARE, Yetta Bernhard tells her reader to say "I count," and describes exactly how to put the premises of self-care into practical, everyday living. 252 pages, soft cover, $6.95

HIDDEN MEANINGS by Dr. Gerald Smith takes Body Language a step further; it defines words and phrases of everyday usage and decodes expressions and tones of voice to reveal the true underlying message. 192 pages, soft cover, $4.95

IT'S UP TO YOU is Eileen D. Gambrill and Cheryl A. Richey's basic handbook for developing assertive social skills. Particular attention is devoted to basics: where to go to meet people, handling conversations, arranging meetings, evaluating contacts and making positive changes. 156 pages, soft cover, $4.95

In THE INWARD JOURNEY, art therapist Margaret Frings Keyes integrates Gestalt techniques with Transactional Analysis and Jungian thought in a rich and illuminating guide for the lay reader to the use of art as therapy. 128 pages, soft cover, $4.95

In HOW TO BE SOMEBODY, noted psychologist Yetta Bernhard presents a specific guide for personal growth that will "lead to acceptance of one's self as a human being." 128 pages, soft cover, $3.95

Available at your local book or department store or directly from the publisher. To order by mail, send check or money order to:

Celestial Arts
231 Adrian Road
Suite MPB
Millbrae, Ca 94030

Please include 50 cents for postage and handling. California residents add 6% tax.